Elisha Jones

METHOD

OF

CLASSICAL STUDY:

ILLUSTRATED BY QUESTIONS

ON A FEW

SELECTIONS FROM LATIN AND GREEK AUTHORS.

BY

SAMUEL H. TAYLOR, LL. D.
PRINCIPAL OF PHILLIPS ACADEMY, ANDOVER, MASS.

BOSTON:
BROWN AND TAGGARD.
25 AND 29 CORNHILL.
1861.

Electrotyped and Printed by W. F. Draper,
Andover, Mass.

PREFACE.

The history of this little volume is briefly told. The author was requested, two or three years since, to furnish some Communications for the "Massachusetts Teacher." One of the Communications furnished was a series of questions on the first seven lines of the Aeneid, and another, similar questions on a few lines of the second Book of the Anabasis. These questions were favorably noticed by several publications, and copies of them were requested by teachers in different parts of the country. From various sources, too, the author was urged to extend the questions, and put them into an accessible form for general use. The result is now given to the public.

The design of the questions is to give illustrations of the various topics of investigation to which attention is to be directed, and to exhibit some of the methods of discussing them. There is a strong tendency among those commencing the study of Latin and Greek, to be satisfied with a few of the more simple and more general principles, and to consider the mastery of these as embracing all that is implied in the study of the classical languages. These questions are designed to give broader views; to spread out the whole field, and show how much is to be done in it. No point that pertains to the fullest acquaintance with a word, or sentence, or the subject in general, should be neglected, so far as the advancement of the student has qualified him to investigate and understand it. The laws by which words have this or that form; why they drop a letter here and assume one there, or change one elsewhere; what part is radical and what accessory; is the word regular or irregular in its formation; has it its primary or secondary sense, and the connection between the one and the other; is it simple or compound, primitive or derivative; its relation to other words, — what it modifies and what modifies it; and the sentence, — is it independent or dependent, substantive, adjective, or adverbial; is its position natural or inverted; the difference between the several declensions and conjugations; why this mode and tense rather than another; all the laws of construction; the circumstances under which the treatise was written; the comparison of Latin with Greek idioms, and these with the English; the synonymes, history, biography, geography, mythology; the logic, rhetoric, poetry, oratory, — all these, with many other subjects, are to be made, at the proper stage, matters of careful study.

The best results of classical study come

only from this broad and critical survey of the whole range of topics. There are treasures in the mine, but it must be patiently and thoroughly worked. Such a method is slow at first; but it gives habits of close observation and analysis, power to reason, and a definite knowledge of fundamental principles, which in the end will make the progress more rapid, and give a better preparation for other courses of study.

The questions are put from various points of view: some are difficult, others quite simple. Some are general, while those that follow are more definite, designed to explain a preceding one. Some take the most abstract or indefinite form, for the purpose of tasking the discrimination of the student. One often contains the answer to another. Some are almost unavoidably leading questions; while others are put in a form likely to mislead the student who determines the answer from the tone of the question, without a careful study of the subject. Sometimes, too, the questions are put in language very different from the usual form, with the view of breaking up a merely mechanical style of answers, which have little significance to the student's mind. Sometimes the question is of such a nature that it at once suggests the answer, though the principle might have been overlooked by the beginner had the question not been asked.

Occasional references are made to the Grammars, — to Andrews and Stoddard's for the Latin, and to Kühner's Elementary Grammar for the Greek, — the figures inclosed in parentheses referring to the sections of these Grammars.[1] The object of these questions did not seem to make the additional references to several other excellent Grammars necessary.

[1] A few changes were made in the last edition of Kühner's Grammar, particularly in sections 8 and 11. The references are to this edition.

A few Notes are added on some of the questions, for the convenience of those who may not have ready access to the requisite sources of information. The small "superior" figures refer to these Notes.

ANDOVER, Oct., 1861.

METHOD OF CLASSICAL STUDY.

QUESTIONS ON THE FIRST FIVE FABLES OF THE LATIN READER.

1. ACCIPĬTER ET COLUMBAE.

Columbae milvii metu accipĭtrem rogavērunt,

At what time is Aesop, the reputed author of these fables, supposed to have lived? Is it certain that the fables which bear his name were written by him? Is there strong evidence that they were not? Did he write in Greek, or Latin? Can it be known certainly who was the author of these fables?

First Fable. In what different cases may the form *columbae* be found? In what case here? How determined? What features of what word does *columbae* determine (209, *b*)? Case of *milvii*? How determined? Why not the subject of *rogaverunt*? By what word governed? Rule (211)? What is meant when it is said to be governed by *metu*? What influence has it on *metu*? Does it make the meaning of *metu* more or less general? What is the design of the termination- or inflection-endings of these nouns, such as *ae* in columbae, *i* in *milvii*, and *u* in *metu*, etc.? The English has no such inflection- or case-

ut eas defendĕret. Ille annuit. At in colum-

endings; how is the defect supplied? How can this be illustrated in the translation of *milvii* and *metu?*[1] What would be the full form of *metu?* Whence comes the *u* (89, R. 1.)? By what principle is *metu* put in the Abl. (247)? What is the meaning of the rule? Does it imply that *metu* is governed by any word?[2] How is *accipĭtrem* governed? Rule (231)? Verbs of asking govern two accusatives, what other accusative does *rogaverunt* take (231 R. 3, *b*)? What would be the full or regular Gen. of *accipiter?* What is the form of the Gen. used? In forming the Gen., what becomes of the *e* in the Nom.? What is the *e* before the *m* in *accipĭtrem?* Has it any meaning? Why used then?[3] What the *m?* How many declensions in the first four words? That of each? What is the characteristic of a declension? What part of *rogaverunt* is root?[4] What is *v*? Subject of *rogaverunt?* What is the connection between a verb and its subject (209, *b*)? What part of speech is *ut?* What is the office of conjunctions (198)? What does *ut* connect? What does it denote here, *purpose, object,* or *result?* What determines the number and gender of *eas* (206 and N. 1)? What determines its case (206)? What conjugation is *defenderet?* What determines the conjugation of a verb? What letter is dropped in the third root of *defenderet?* Why?[5] Why in the subjunctive? What letter inserted before *t* of *defenderet* would make it third Pers. Pl.? How else can *ut defenderet* be translated into English besides *that he would defend?* Can *ut,* with the subjunctive, denoting

bāre receptus, uno die majōrem stragem edĭdit, quàm milvius longo tempŏre potuisset edĕre.

purpose, or *object*, be often translated into English by *to* with the Inf.? What kind of a pronoun is *ille* (134)? Is it properly ever a substantive personal pronoun?[6] How many substantive personal pronouns are there (133)? What are they? Is "he assented" a full translation of *ille annuit?* Why not? What is not indicated by that translation? Is "he assented" right as far as it goes? What tense is *annuit?* What is the difficulty in determining? In what two places can it be made? What different cases does *in* govern? When one, and when the other (235, 2)? Declension of *columbare?* Case? How determined? Gender? Rule (66)? What is the Abl. Sing. (82, Exc. 1, *a*)? What is the *re* in *receptus* (196, *b*)? Does it ever stand alone? Composition of *receptus?* What would be the form if *re* were omitted,—*ceptus* or *captus?* What participle is *receptus?* What different participles have verbs? How many active, and how many passive? What determines the gender and number of *receptus?* Rule (205)? In what two cases is *unus* irregular in its declension? What other words have a Gen. like *unus* (107)? Declension of *die?* Gender? Same in Sing. and Pl.? What would be the full form?[7] Is the *e* long, or short? How comes it so? By what principle is *die* in the Abl.? What would be the unabbreviated form instead of *majorem?* What becomes of *n* of the positive? Of *g?* Does the *n* belong to the root? Gender of *majorem?* How determined? Why not by its form (109 and

Fabŭla docet, malōrum patrocinium vitandum esse.

110)? What peculiarity has *edidit* in its second root (163, Rem.)? How many simple verbs have this peculiarity in Latin?[8] What is the root of *edidit?* What is the root of a verb (150, 1)? We call *quam* a conjunction, — what part of speech is it strictly, and in what case? What is its office here, *i. e.*, what does it connect? What relation does the clause following *quam* sustain to the preceding one?[9] Comparative and superlative of *longo?* What is the object of having different degrees of comparison? When the comparative is used, how many objects are compared (122, 5)? Does the use of the superlative determine how many objects are compared (122, 6)? Is it always more than two? Root or stem of *tempore?* Nom.? How is the stem of a noun of the third Dec. found?[10] Construction of *tempore* (236)? Is it governed by any word? Does the rule mean anything more than that, when a noun denotes the relation here indicated, it is put in the Acc. or Abl. case? Composition of *potuisset* (154, R. 7)? Full form instead of *potuisset?* If the Perf. of *sum* is *fui*, what would be the full Perf. of *possum?* Why does the first *s* of *possum* become *t* in the Perf. What changed the *t* of *pot* to *s* in *possum?* Is there any such influence in the Perf. to change it? Why *potuisset* in the subjunctive[11] (260, II.)? Government or construction of *edere* (271)? What is meant by a fable? How is *malorum* used here (205, R. 7, 1)? How compared? What connection between the positive *malus* and the forms of the compara-

2. MUS ET MILVIUS.

Milvius laqueis irretītus muscŭlum exorāvit,

tive and superlative?[12] Construction of *patrocinium* (239)? Of what is *patrocinium* the subject-accusative? What particle must the English supply in translating the Acc. with the Inf., which is not expressed in Latin (273)? What case does the Acc. before the Inf. become in English? After what class of verbs is the Acc. with the Inf. used (272)? What is the force of the Part. in *dus* (274, R. 8)? What kind of a conjugation is *esse vitandum* (162, 15)?

Second Fable. Construction of *laqueis* (247)? Does the rule imply that this and words similarly constructed are governed by any word, or that the nouns expressing the cause, manner, means, etc., are put in the Abl. to denote these relations? Composition of the verb from which *irretitus* comes? How does the first *r* in the word originate[13] (196, 7)? What Part. is *irretitus*? Has the Latin any Perf. Act. Part.? With what does *irretitus* agree? Rule (205)? What kind of a noun is *musculum*? From what is the diminutive formed? What are the endings of diminutives (100, 3)? What part of *exoravit* is simple root?[4] What is the *v*? *i*? *t*? Force of *ex*? When is *ex* used in composition, and when *e* (195, R. 2)? Is *exoravit* the Perf. definite or indefinite? What tenses follow the Perf. indefinite, or historical Perf. (258, 2, et seq.)? What does *ut* connect? Rule? In what different ways can *ut* with the subjunctive be here translated? From what does *eum* come? How many declensions in *is*? The masculine and neuter are of what

ut eum, corrōsis plagis, liberāret. Quo facto,

declension? The feminine of what? Would *se* answer as well as *eum* here? Why not (208)? What would *se* mean? From what verb does *corrosis* come? Composition? How does the first *r* originate?[13] What letter is dropped in the second and third root of the verb?[5] Why? Declension of *plagis*? Construction? What is meant by the term *Abl. absolute*? What relations does the Abl. absolute express (257)? What is the relation here? *Corrosis plagis* may be rendered three ways: "the nets having been gnawed," "having gnawed the nets," "by gnawing the nets,"—which is literal? Which the best? In what feature does the Latin and English differ, that, in such expressions as *corrosis plagis*, the Perf. Pass. Part. may generally be rendered by our Perf. Act. Part., and the Abl. as governed by it; *i. e.*, "having gnawed the nets?"[14] Does the *a* in *liberaret* belong to the root or not?[4] Do verbs of the first conjugation exhibit the full form, or is there a contraction? Why *liberaret* in the subjunctive? If *exoravit* had been in the Pres. tense, in what tense would *liberaret* have been? What is the principle for the connection of tenses (258, I.) Is *quo* masculine or neuter? How determined (206, 13)? Has *quo* here the same force as *hoc*?[15] What is the difference? How may the difference be expressed in English (280, III. 1)? Will our particle of transition *now* indicate it? Construction of *quo*? What relation does the Abl. absolute express here (257)? Is it that of time or cause? In the expression *corrosis plagis* above, where *plagis* is in the Abl. absolute

milvius liberātus murem arripuit et devorāvit.

with the Perf. Pass. Part., it was seen that it could be translated into English, "having gnawed the nets," — can *quo facto* be translated "having done which or this"? Why not? Was the action denoted by *corrosis plagis* performed by the same agent (the mouse) as that indicated by *liberaret?* But was the action denoted by *quo facto* performed by the same agent as that denoted by *arripuit?* Who performed the act denoted by *quo facto?* When, then, can a Perf. Pass. Part., standing in the Abl. absolute with a noun or pronoun, be translated into English by our Perf. Act. Part.?[16] From what does *facto* come? What is the Nom. of *murem?* Root? What is the *s* in *mus?*[17] What influence has it on the *r* (*mur*) of the root?[18] What is the *e* in *murem?* The *m?* Does *murem* denote the same object as *musculum?* Why is not a specific word used in the second instance as well as in the first? Can there be any doubt after one specific designation? Composition of *arripuit?* Force of the preposition? By what principle is the *d* of the preposition changed into *r*[19] (196, 2)? Composition of *devoravit?* Force of *de?* What determines the gender and number of *haec?* Composition of *ostendit?* What becomes of the *b* of the preposition?[20] What two features of *ostendit* does *fabula* determine? Rule? What letter of *ostendit* is dropped in the third root, and why?[5] Does *quam* come from *quis* or *qui?* How determined (137, 1)?[21] *Ostendit* is a transitive verb, — what does it govern here? May a clause or sentence stand as the subject or object of a verb?

Haec fabŭla ostendit, quam gratiam mali pro beneficiis reddĕre soleant.

3. HOEDUS ET LUPUS.

Hoedus, stans in tecto domûs, lupo praeter-

Is such sentence declinable or indeclinable? Government of *gratiam?* *Mali* how used here (205, R. 7)? What case does *pro* govern? What two cases do Latin prepositions govern? How many the Acc. (195, 4)? How many the Abl. (195, 5)? Do any Latin prepositions govern more than one case (195, 6)? What? How is it determined which case is to be used (235)? Why are prepositions so called (195, R. 1)? Composition of *beneficiis?* Of *reddere?* Is *re* ever found alone? What is the *d* that is sometimes added to *re?* What is meant by a paragogic letter (322, 6)? When is *d* added (196, *b*, 3)? Why? Is it added in this word according to rule, or by exception? What peculiarity in the second root of *reddere* (163, R.)? Upon what does *reddere* depend (271)? What kind of a verb is *soleant* (142, 2)? Why so called? Why in the subjunctive? If *n* be removed from *soleant,* where will the word be made? What, then, is *n* the sign of?

Third Fable. Of which conjugation is *stans?* Perf. Act. of its verb? What two irregularities in that tense?[22] Is reduplication common in Latin? When is the vowel of reduplication (*i. e.* the vowel after the first consonant of the Perf.) *e?*[23] Can it be determined whether *tecto* is in the Dat. or Abl. here? How? Why is *in* here followed by the Abl.? What declension is *domûs?*

eunti maledixit. Cui lupus, "Non tu," inquit, "sed tectum mihi̯ maledīcit."

Is it of more than one declension? Is it in the Nom. or Gen.? How determined, independent of the mark over the Gen. which does not belong to the word? Is there any way for disposing of it in the Nom.? How can it be disposed of in the Gen.? *i. e.*, how can it be parsed? Would the Gen. *domi* have been as proper here? Why not (89, *a*)? The ending *us* in *domus* is a contraction from what (89, R. 1)? In what case is *lupo*? How can it be determined whether it is Dat. or Abl.? Is there any principle by which it can be parsed in the Abl.? What for putting it in the Dat. (225)? Composition of *praetereunti*? When do the forms of *eo* begin with *e*, and when with *i*?[24] Is it so in the Pres. Part.? Why not? Would the form *eens* (two *e*'s), be as euphonic as *iens*? But when the penult *e* of the Nom. changes to *u* in the Gen. etc., what becomes of the *i* that was in the Nom.? Composition of *maledixit*? What two letters form the *x* (3, 2)? Is *cui* from *quis* or *qui*? How determined? How governed? What does *non* qualify? Rule (277)? Of what is *tu* the subject? Can it be the subject of *maledicit*? Why not? What has determined the form of *maledicit* (209, R. 12, 7, *a*)? When two nominatives of different persons are subjects of the same verb, does the second or the third person commonly determine the form of the verb (209, R. 12, 7)? Is it so here? What kind of a verb is *inquit* (183, 2)? Its subject here? What is its general position in introducing a quotation (279, 6)? *Saepe* how compared? What pe-

Saepe locus et tempus homīnes timīdos audāces reddit.

4. GRUS ET PAVO.

Pavo, coram grue pennas suas explĭcans,

culiarity has *locus* in the Pl. (92, I. 2)? What are such nouns called? Meaning of *loca*, and *loci*? Stem of *tempus*? What change from the stem takes place in forming the Nom.? Where does the stem appear? Stem of *homines*? Construction? What other Acc. is governed by the same word? Rule (230)? Which word is the Acc. of the object, and which of the predicate? Of what Dec. is *timidos*? What *audaces*? How many endings has each? Stem of *audaces*? How from the stem *audac* is the Nom. *audax* formed? Origin of the first *d* in *reddit*? Where the vowel of the reduplication in simple verbs is *e*, is it the same in compounds? What is that vowel in *do*? What in *reddo* (compare *sto* and *consto*, etc.)? On what principle is *reddit* singular, having two subjects?

Fourth Fable. What letter in the stem of *pavo* is rejected in the Nom.?[25] Where does the rejected letter appear? What part of speech is *coram* here? Is it always a preposition? How determined to be here? As *suas* refers to *pavo* why is it not singular? When an adjective pronoun agrees with a noun must it be in the same number as the noun, whatever be the number of the word to which the adjective pronoun refers (205)? Why is *suas* used and not *ejus* (208)? Can the English distinguish by the translation the difference between *suas* and *ejus*? Pecu-

"Quanta est," inquit, "formosĭtas mea et tua deformĭtas?" At grus evŏlans, "Et quanta est," inquit, "levĭtas mea et tua tardĭtas!"

Monet haec fabŭla, ne ob alĭquod bonum,

liarity in the second and third roots of *explicavit?* What is the form of the Pres. before contraction takes place? Force of *ex* in composition? Meaning of *quantus* when it agrees with a noun? When it is in the neuter gender and governs a Gen.?[26] What are the subjects of *est?* Why not in the Pl. then? How does the *e* in *est* come from the form *sum?*[27] Stem of *formositas?* What letter excludes or rejects the final *t* of the stem? What is the *s* appended to the stem?[17] Why does *mea* stand after *formositas,* but *tua* before *deformitas?* What is the position of similar and contrasted words in a sentence?[28] Is *at* a stronger or weaker adversative than *sed?* Is *autem* stronger or weaker than *sed*[29] (198, 9, R. *a*)? Force of *e* in *evolans?* Why *e* and not *ex?* Stems of *levitas* and *tarditas?* Does the same principle hold in regard to the position of *mea* and *tua* with these words as above? *Monet* being a transitive verb governs an object in the Acc., — what is that object here? What does *ne* connect (278)? Why is *ne* used here rather than *non* (260, R. 6, *a* and *b*)? How is *aliquod* declined? Any difference between *aliquod* and *aliquid* (138, 2, *b*)? Which is used as an adjective and which as a substantive? Is *bonum* here a substantive or an adjective? What determines the gender, number and person of *quod* (206)? What determines its case? In what two cases might it be in form? What is the case of *nobis?* How

quod nobis natūra tribuit, alios contemnāmus, quibus natūra alia et fortasse majōra dedit.

5. PAVO.

Pavo gravīter conquerebātur apud Junōnem,

determined? Is there any principle by which it could be disposed of in the Abl. here? Is *nobis* the direct or indirect object of *tribuit?* What is the direct object? Is *tribuit* in the Pres. or Perf. tense? Can that be determined by the form? Is *alios* here an adjective or a substantive? What is its Gen. Sing.? Any other words with a Gen. Sing. in the same form? Why *contemnamus* in the subjunctive (273, 2)? Does the second *n* in *contemnamus* belong to the root?[30] Peculiarity in the second and third root of the word?[31] Why is the *p* inserted in these two roots? Antecedent of *quibus?* Of what person is it? How determined? From what positive does *major* come? Root of the positive? What has become of the *n* of the positive? What of the *g?* Whence comes the *j?*[32] Were the *i* and *j* ever expressed by the same sign? Do *alia* and *majora* agree with anything here? The Pres. of *dedit?* When is the vowel of the reduplication *e?*

Fifth Fable. Comparison of *graviter?* From what adjective formed? Force of *con* in *conquerebatur?* In the Part. *conquestus,* what becomes of the *r* of the Pres.?[33] Force of the Impf. *conquerebatur?* Stem of *Junonem?* What previous word like it? What is the *e* in *Junonem?* The *m?* Construction of *dominam?* What is its office here (204, R. 1)? Why *suam* and not *ejus?* Is *quod* here

domĭnam suam, quod vocis suavĭtas sibi negāta esset, dum luscinia, avis tam parum decōra, cantu excellat. Cui Juno, "Et merĭtò," in-

a conjunction or a relative? What was it originally? What does it connect here? Stem of *vocis*? How from the stem is the Nom. *vox* formed?[34] What is the *i* in *vocis*? What word does *vocis* define or explain? When it is said to be governed by *suavitas* what is meant? Is *sua* in *suavitas* one or two syllables (9, 4)? Why *sibi* and not *ei*? Composition of *nego* from which *negata esset* comes? Why *esset* in the subjunctive? Is *quod* in the sense of *because* always followed by the subjunctive? When (266, 3)? What English clause can be inserted after *quod* to indicate that the sentiment here is not that of the writer? Would "as she said" indicate that fact? Can a clause of similar import generally be inserted where the statement following *quod* is that of some other person than the writer? Whose sentiment does *negata esset* express here? What does *tam* qualify? What *parum*? How is *parum* compared? From what verb is *cantu* derived? Of which declension? Why Abl.? Why *excellat* in the subjunctive? For the same reason as *negata esset*? Can "as she said" be inserted after *dum* also, as after *quod* above? Government of *cui*? What does *merito* qualify, — a word in this sentence, or in the preceding one? Rule for the position of *inquit*? What is the usual position of *enim* in a sentence? Is that of *nam* the same (198, 7, R.)? What declension is *omnia*? *Bona*? Construction of *bona* (239)? On what does the Inf. *conferri* depend (273, 4, *a*,)? Why is *in* here followed by the

quit; "non enim omnia bona in unum conferri oportuit."

Acc.? Gen. Sing. of *unum*? What kind of a verb is *oportuit*? What is meant by an impersonal verb (184)?

NEPOS.

QUESTIONS ON THE FIRST CHAPTER OF MILTIADES.

MILTIADES, Cimonis filius, Atheniensis, quum

WHO was the author of these Lives. Where was he born? With what distinguished literary men was he contemporary? Did he write anything besides these Lives? Are these probably in the form he wrote them?

Is *Miltiades* the family name, as when we say *Webster*, or the personal name, as when we say *Daniel?* Why does the name *Miltiades* stand alone with no other name, and so Themistocles, Aristides, etc., while the persons described in the two last Lives of Nepos have two additional names: M. Portius Cato, and T. Pomponius Atticus? Of what nation were Miltiades, Themistocles, etc., Greek or Roman? Of what Cato and Atticus. Had the Greeks any family or surnames?[1] How was it with the Romans? With which of the names Marcus Portius Cato does Miltiades correspond? Would it be proper then to say, in speaking of these two persons: Was Miltiades superior to Marcus? Why not as admissible in the one case as the other? Was the name Marcus confined to Cato, or was it used as the name of others also? Was the same true to any extent of Miltiades, and other Greek names?

et antiquitate generis, et gloria majorum, et

Declension of *Miltiades*? Construction? Is it the subject of any verb?[2] Root of *Cimonis*? Government? What is meant when *Cimonis* is said to be governed by *filius*, *i. e.* what is the office of this Gen.? Vocative of *filius*? Is that the usual form of the Voc. of common nouns in *-ius* (52)? Construction of *filius*? What is the office of a noun in apposition (204, R. 1, *a*)? Is *Atheniensis* a noun or adjective? How constructed? What other form the same as *quum*? How is *cum* formed from *quum*?[3] What does *quum* connect? Is it *floreret* and *judicarunt*, or *floreret* and *accidit*? What is the office of *et* before *antiquitate*? Does it connect anything? What would be lost if it were omitted? Would the statement or fact be different if *et* were omitted?[4] How can its force be expressed in English? In any other way? To what word is *et* after *quum* related? What is that relation?[5] If the first *et* is translated *both*, how will the second be translated? If the first, *not only*, how the second? Would good Latin usage allow the three *et*'s to be omitted here? Could the first two be omitted and the third retained?[6] Derivation of *antiquitate*? Root? Nom. how formed? Construction of *antiquitate*? Is it governed by any word? What restricts or defines its meaning? Root or stem of *generis*? What change from the root in forming the Nom.? In what case does the root appear? Does the Gen. stand before or after the word by which it is governed? Can any uniform rule be given for its position?[7] What does *et* before *gloria* connect? Rule? What is the positive of *majorum*? Root

sua modestia unus omnium maxime floreret, eaque esset aetate, ut jam non solum de eo

of *magnus?* Is *majorum* a noun or an adjective? How does it come to mean *ancestors?* What word is understood with it? Origin of the *j* in *majorum?*[8] Why is *sua* used here and not *ejus* (208)? Derivation of *modestia?* Its meaning here? What word expresses its opposite? Gen. of *unus?* What other words have the same form in the Gen.? Force of *unus* here? What word is strengthened by it (127, N. 2)? Upon what word does the force of *omnium* fall, *i. e.*, what word does it strengthen? Upon what word does the combined force of *unus omnium* fall?[9] How will the clause be translated if *unus omnium* is omitted? How if *omnium?* How as it is now written? Construction of *omnium?* Rule (212)? Could *omnium* be omitted without any loss to the expression? The origin of *x* in *maxime?*[10] Of which conjugation is *floreret?* What determines to which conjugation a verb belongs? How comes the penult of the Inf. Act. of the second conjugation to be long, when the penult *e* of the Pres. Indic. (as *docĕo*, *florĕo*, etc.) is always short?[11] Why *floreret* in the subjunctive (263, R. 2)? Why in the Impf.? Its subject? Meaning of *ea* here? The office of *que?* How differing from *et* (198, II., 1, R. *a*)? Does *que* ever stand alone? What is it called then (198, N. 1)? How is *esset* formed from *sum?*[12] Construction of *aetate* (211, R. 6)? From what noun does *aetate* come? The Nom. *aetas* a contraction from what? What does *ut* connect? Is it always followed by the subjunctive? When is it (262, et seq.)?

2*

bene sperare, sed etiam confidere cives possent

Force of *jam?* How differing from *nunc* (277, R. 15)?[13] In the formula *non solum——sed etiam,* is the transition from the less important to the more important, or the reverse (277, R. 10)? What is the formula when the transition is from the greater to the less? Between what words does *de* show the relation? What is the office of prepositions (195)? *Bene* from what adjective, — *benus* or *bonus?* With what change if from the latter? Why is *bene* needed with *sperare?* Is *sperare* generally taken in a good sense, *i. e.*, hoping for something good? Is it ever used in the sense of fear? May the idea of something good in *sperare* be strengthened by *bene?* Whence comes the *a* in *sperare*, and why long?[11] Composition of *etiam?* Force of *con* in *confidere?* Does this verb form all its parts regularly? What kind of a verb is it (142, 2)? Why so called? What letter is dropped in the third root? Is *d* regularly dropped before *s?* Upon what do *sperare* and *confidere* depend? Rule (271)? Does the word *cives* here mean citizens, or fellow-citizens? Was the word *concivis* in use in the best period of the language? Origin of the first *s* in *possent?* Why *possent* in the subjunctive? Is it sufficient to say after *ut?* Why not? Is such a rule ever admissible? Does the Indicative also occur after *ut?* Is it any rule at all then to say that a verb is in the subjunctive after *ut?* What rule should be given (262, with R. 1)? What two words of this sentence does *ut* connect? What is the *n* in *possent?* If it is removed, what will the form be? Why *sui* here and not *eorum?* With what does *talem* agree?

sui, talem futurum, qualem cognitum judicarunt: accidit, ut Athenienses Chersonesum co-

What connection has *futurum* with *sum*? What is understood with it? Is *esse* very frequently omitted with the Fut. Inf.? Upon what does *futurum* [*esse*] depend? Rule for the Acc. with the Inf. here (272)? What are *talis* and *qualis*, and words similarly related called (139, 5, 2)? What is the proper meaning of *qualis*? When *talis* precedes, how is *qualis* to be translated into English? Can the second correlative (as *tantus, quantus, tot, quot,* etc.) be usually so translated? Composition of *cognitum*? Force of the preposition? Whence comes the *g*?[14] What is the root of the last part of the compound? The origin of *sc* in *nosco*?[15] How may the force of the Perf. Part. *cognitum* be here expressed? What is the full form for *judicarunt*? When may such contraction take place, and how (162, 7)? Is *judicarunt* the Perf. definite or indefinite? Is *accidit* Pres. or Perf. tense? Any difference in the form? How is it to be determined then? If *accidit* were Pres., according to the rule for the connection of tenses (258), in what tense would *vellent* be? *Vellent* being in the Impf., what is the inference as to the tense of *accidit*? How does *accidit* differ from *evĕnit, contingit*? What kind of a noun is *Athenienses* (100, 2)? What does a patrial noun denote? How are patrials formed (128, 6)? Are patrials generally nouns or adjectives (100, N. 3)? What does *ut* before *Athenienses* connect? Construction of *Chersonesum* (237)? But is this the name of a town or of a small island? Does it, however, in its construction, follow

lonos vellent mittere. 2. Cujus generis quum magnus numerus esset, et multi ejus demigrationis peterent societatem: ex his delecti Del-

the construction of small islands (237, R. 5, *b*)? Is it proper to say that it is governed by anything? What Chersonesus is denoted? Why is it not specified? What is a Chersonese? What English word is its equivalent? Composition of the word? Derivation of *colonos?* What would have been the regular form instead of *vellent?* By what changes is this form obtained (178, R.)? What is the *n* in *vellent?* From the Pres. *mitto* how comes the Perf. *mīsi?*[16] How *missum?* Why does *cujus* stand at the head of the sentence?[17] Derivation of *generis?* Stem from which the Nom. is formed? What change for the formation of the Nom.?[18] What word is restricted or explained by *generis?* Whence the first *e* in *esset?* The second *s?*[19] The root of *sum* from which *esset* comes? Why the subjunctive? Wherein is *multi* irregular in its comparison? Have the comparative and superlative any relation to the positive in form? What does *et* connect? Rule (278)? What are the similar constructions here? Force of the preposition *de* in *demigrationis?* How is the relation of this Gen. expressed in English? Is the relation of the Gen. always denoted by *of?*[20] Peculiarity in the second and third roots of *peterent?*[21] What kind of a noun is *societatem* (26, 5)? Derivation? Stem? What rejects the final *t* of the stem? What is the *s* thus appended to the stem called? Difference between *e* and *ex?* What does *ex* show the relation between here? By what eupho-

phos deliberatum missi sunt, qui consulerent Apollinem, quo potissimum duce uterentur. Namque tum Thraces eas regiones tenebant,

nic principle does the *g* of *deligo* become *c* in *delecti*?[22] How is *delecti* used here? *Delphi* where? Declension and number? For what celebrated? Construction? Composition of *deliberatum*? In its primary sense? What part of speech? Active or passive? What would be the Pass. form? By what principle is the supine used here (276, II.)? What part of *sunt* is root? What is the *u*? *n*? *t*? What word determines three features of *qui*? What are the three features (206)? What two features of what word does *qui* determine (209, *b*)? Why *consulerent* in the subjunctive (264, 5)? What mode of expression could be substituted for *qui*, giving the same meaning? Grammatical object of *consulerent*? Stem of *Apollinem*? Nom.? How from the stem is the Nom. formed?[23] Construction of *quo*? Has it any antecedent? Why not? Is it a relative or interrogative pronoun? *Duce* from what verb? Stem? Nom. how formed?[24] Construction (204, R. 1)? *Uterentur* why in the subjunctive (265)? What letter is dropped in the Perf. Part. of *utor*? On what principle? What part of *uterentur* exhibits the corresponding mode and tense of the Active? What is the *u* after the *t*? What the *r*?[25] Where was *Thrace*? What place is referred to by *eas regiones*? Force of the Impf. *tenebant*? How else could *cum quibus* be written (241, R. 1)? Antecedent of *quibus*? Does its form determine whether it is *Thraces* or *regiones*? Does the position of

cum quibus armis erat dimicandum. 3. His consulentibus nominatim Pythia praecepit, ut

these words determine which is the antecedent? How can it be decided? Construction of *armis?* Different applications or meanings of the word? Is it used in the Sing.? Difference between it and *tela?* Which is offensive and which defensive weapons? What conjugation is *erat dimicandum* (162, 15)? How used here, *i. e.* what is its subject? What class of verbs is always used impersonally in the passive (142, 1)?[26] Why? Why does *his* stand at the beginning of the sentence?[17] Construction? Is it in the Dat. or Abl.? May it not be in the Abl. absolute with *consulentibus?* Would the form of either of the words determine that? What does determine the construction of *his?* By what principle does it depend on *praecepit* (223, R. 2)? Meaning of *consulo* when it governs an Acc. (as *consulo te*)? When it governs a Dat. (as *consulo tibi*)? Derivation of *nominatim?* *Nomino* from what? *Nomen* from what? What connection between *nomen* and *nosco?* What is a *nomen?* Is it not that by which anything is *known?* Who was *Pythia?* Derivation? Is the word strictly a substantive or an adjective? Composition of *praecepit?* In the Pres. what change takes place in the last part of the compound? How is the *e* in *praecepit* to be explained, it being *i* in the Pres. (172, *capio*)? What becomes of the *i* in the inflection of the Pres. Indic. Act. and Pass. of *capio?*[27] In what form of the Pres. Act. and Pass., however, is the *i* retained? Does the *i* belong to the root or is it merely a strengthening letter? What does *ut*

Miltiadem sibi imperatorem sumerent: id si fecissent, incepta prospera futura. 4. Hoc oraculi responso Miltiades cum delecta manu

connect? Why is it here followed by a past tense and not by a present? Construction of *sibi?* What kind of a pronoun is it? Is it singular or plural? How determined? To what does it refer? Could *iis* be substituted for it? Why? Is *imperatorem* strictly in apposition with *Miltiadem?* What is its construction (230)? How can *ut* with the subjunctive here be rendered? Why *sumerent* in the subjunctive? Is it sufficient to say that it is in the subjunctive after *ut?* Why not? Is *sumerent* a simple or compound verb? Origin of *p* in the second and third root?[28] To what does *id* refer? Why in neuter gender (206, 13)? What does *si* connect? In *oratio recta,* in what mode and tense would *fecissent* have been (266, 2, R. 4)? Does the word here express past or future time? What relation of future time? What relation of time does the action of *fecissent* sustain to that of *futura?* Do they both relate to future time? Which is prior to the other? Composition of *incepta?* Construction? Is it Nom. or Acc.? Composition of *prospera?* Is it an attributive or predicative adjective. What is understood with *futura?* Upon what does the Inf. *futura* [*esse*] depend (270, R. 2, *b*)? In what mode and tense would it have been in *oratio recta?*[29] Why *hoc* at the first of the sentence? Derivation of *oraculi?* What word does it restrict or define? Derivation of *responso?* Construction (249, II.)? Is it governed by any word, or simply put in the Abl. to denote

classe Chersonesum profectus quum accessisset Lemnum, et incolas ejus insulae sub potestatem redigere vellet Atheniensium, idque Lemnii

the relation intended? How is the *c* in *delecta* to be explained?[22] Gender of *manu?* Is that the gender of most nouns in *us* of the fourth Dec. (87)? Primary meaning of *classe?* Since the word *Chersonesus* has a general meaning (a *Chersonese* or *peninsula*), how can it be determined what particular place is meant? By what principle in the Acc.? From what verb does *profectus* come? Composition of *proficiscor?* What syllable is inserted in the Pres.?[30] In what parts of the verb is that syllable retained? When is *sc* and when *isc* inserted in the Pres.? What does *quum* connect? Origin of the first of the two *c*'s and the first of the two *s*'s in *accessisset* (196, 2 and 171, 3)? Why *accessisset* in the subjunctive (263, 5, R. 2)? In what sea was *Lemnos*, and in what part? Construction of *Lemnum?* What does *et* connect? Rule? Composition of *incolas?* What cases does *sub* govern? When one and when the other (235, 2)? Derivation of *potestatem?* Stem? Nom.? What rejects the *t* in the Nom.? What kind of a noun is *potestatem*, abstract or concrete (26, 5)? Composition of *redigere?* What is the *d*, and why used here (196, *b*, 3)? Does the *a* of *ago* always become *i* in composition, as here (172, *ago*)? Government of *redigere* (271)? Why *vellet* in the Impf., while *accessisset* is Plupf.? Origin of the second *l* in *vellet?* To what does *id* refer? Why neuter? What does *que* after *id* connect? Why *sua* and not *eorum?* Construction of *sponte?* Is *sua sponte* or

sua sponte facerent, postulasset: 5. illi irridentes responderunt, tum id se facturos, quum ille, domo navibus proficiscens vento aquilone,

sponte sua used indifferently?[31] On what principle is *facerent* in the subjunctive? What connective is omitted before it? With words of what signification is *ut* omitted (262, R. 4)? Full form of *postulasset?* How does the syncopation take place (162, 7, *a*)? Why in *postulasset* does the writer return again to the Plupf.? What is its grammatical object? Why subjunctive? Composition of *irridentes?* On what principle is the *n* of *in* changed into *r* (196, 7)? Does *in* when compounded with a verb have a negative or intensive force?[32] What when compounded with an adjective? What word does *tum* qualify? With what word is it correlative? Does the English generally use two such words, or does it omit the antecedent one, *i. e.* does it say *then* — *when*, or simply *when*, where the clauses are near together? Why *se* and not *eos?* Construction of *se?* What class of verbs have an Acc. with an Inf. after them (272)? What is understood with *facturos?* What Inf. is *facturos* [*esse*]? What form would *facturos* take in *oratio recta?*[33] Construction of *domo* (255, R. 1)? Of what two declensions is *domus?* Construction of *navibus* (247)? Origin of *v* in it? In *proficiscens* how much is root? What syllable is inserted? As *proficiscor* has no active form, how is the existence of a Pres. Act. Part. *proficiscens* to be explained? Have deponent verbs generally all the participles (161)? Construction of *vento?* What wind is meant by *aquilone?* Is the first *e* in *venisset* long

venisset Lemnum. Hic enim ventus, ab septentrionibus oriens, adversum tenet Athenis proficiscentibus. 6. Miltiades, morandi tempus non habens, cursum direxit, quo tendebat, pervenitque Chersonesum.

or short? By what principle is it so (284, Exc. 1)? Why *venisset* in the subjunctive? What mode and tense would it be in *oratio recta?* How, then, would *id se facturos, quum venisset Lemnum* stand in *oratio recta?* In what person would each of the verbs be? Usual position of *enim* in a sentence (198, 7, R. *a*)? *Nam?* Difference between *nam* and *enim?* What does *ab* show the relation between? What meaning has it with verbs of rest? Can it be translated by *in* here? But does *in* express the view as it lay in the mind of a Roman, or is it merely the English mode of expression? How does *septentriones* come to signify the North? What is the primary meaning? Where was the constellation denoted by the word? Composition? By what principle does the *m* of *septem* (the first part of the compound) become *n?*[34] From what does *oriens* come? How can *oriens*, an active participle, come from a verb which has no active form? With what does *adversum* agree? Construction of *Athenis?* Is it governed by any word? Is it used in the singular? From what does *morandi* come? Do deponent verbs have the gerunds and supines as well as all the participles (161 and paradigm)? Composition of *direxit?* The elements which form the *x* (171, 1)? Why *tendebat* in the Impf., while *direxit* and *pervenit* are in the Perf.?

CICERO.

QUESTIONS ON THE FIRST CHAPTER OF THE FIRST ORATION AGAINST CATILINE.

QUOUSQUE tandem abutere, Catilina, patien-

What is the full name of Catiline? What part of the name was *Lucius?* What *Sergius?* Was he a patrician or plebeian? Had he in any way been connected with Sulla? What had been the effect of Sulla's career upon him? Is it likely that he would have attempted the conspiracy if he had not been familiar with Sulla's character and success? Had he held any offices in the state? What? What had been his conduct in Africa? In what year did he return to Rome? For what purpose? Was he a candidate for the consulship the next year after his return? Why not? Of what crime had he been accused? Was he acquitted? By what means? Had he been guilty of any more private crimes? Were his associates in the conspiracy rich or poor? What was the chief object of the conspiracy? Was the wealth at this time in the hands of the many or the few? Were the revolutionists mostly in debt? Were any of them of patrician rank?

Was Cicero of patrician or plebeian rank? Was he popular with the nobility? At what age did he deliver this oration? What office did he hold at the time? How

tia nostra? Quamdiu etiam furor iste tuus

long had he held it? Who was the other consul the same year? Had Catiline been a candidate for the same office that year? Did he come near an election? In what year B. C. was this oration delivered? What month? What day of the month? Before the senate or the people? In what place was the senate convened? Was that the usual place? Why the change at this time? What two circumstances explain the abruptness with which the oration commences? Cicero's feelings having been long exasperated by the course of Catiline, and long restrained, how would he be likely to speak when the restraint was removed? Did Cicero expect that Catiline would be present that day at the meeting of the senate? What effect, then, would the effrontery of his unexpected appearance have upon the style of the orator? Is this properly an oration or an invective?

Composition of *quousque*? Of *tandem*? By what principle does *m* of *tam* become *n*?[1] What is the *dem*?[2] What is the office of *tandem* here, or what does it add to the expression? When does it give emphasis to the expression with which it is connected?[3] What other form could be used besides *abutere*? Is the form in *-re* usual in the second Pers. Pres. Indic. Pass. (162, 3)? Why not?[4] Force of *ab* in *abutere*? How had Catiline trifled with or trampled upon their patience? Had the forbearance of the senate corrected or increased his reckless spirit? Derivation of *patientia*? Primary meaning? Who is meant by *nostra*, Cicero merely, or the senate and consuls? Composition of *etiam*? Force and meaning? Does it simply

nos eludet? Quem ad finem sese effrenata

append an additional consideration (*moreover*, *also*), or has it a relation of time (*still*, *yet*)? What peculiar fitness has the word *furor* here?[5] From what is the picture or figure indicated by *eludet* derived?[6] To what expedient of the gladiator to avoid the blow of his antagonist is there reference? Composition of *iste*?[7] What principle is observable in the position of *iste* and *tuus*?[8] *Iste* how differing from *ille* or *is* (207, R. 25 and 26)? Has it primarily either a good or a bad sense? What circumstance has given it often a bad sense (207, R. 25)?[9] To what person does it generally refer? Can the English distinguish, in translation, between *is* and *ille*, except by a periphrasis? Can the distinction be made in the passage here? Second and third root of *eludet*? What becomes of the *d* in these roots? Does *quem* come from *quis* or *qui*? What is the general difference between *quis* and *qui* as interrogatives?[10] Does *quem ad finem* refer to place or time? Does it mean anything different from *quamdiu*? Does it always have this latter signification in Cicero?[11] What peculiarity in the form of *sese* (133, R. 2)?[12] What is the object of that peculiarity? Is any other case reduplicated besides the Acc.? Were any other words than *sese* at any period of the language reduplicated? Has *sese* any Nom.? Why not? Composition of *effrenata*? Origin of the first *f* (196, 6)? From what is the metaphor implied in this word derived? Root of *jactabit*? What is the *b*? *i*? *t*? What kind of a verb is *jacto*? From what simple verb? Of which conjugation are frequentative verbs (187, II. 1,

jactabit audacia? Nihilne te nocturnum praesidium Palatii, nihil urbis vigiliae, nihil timor

a)? What do such verbs denote? Derivation of *audacia?* What letters are added to the root of the adjective to form the noun? Are *furor* and *audacia* here used as abstract qualities, or are they personified (324, 34)? Composition of *nihil?* Meaning of each part? Is it a substantive or adjective? In what case? By what principle (231, R. 5)? What is the *ne* appended to *nihil* (198, II, R. *c*)? What is its usual place (279, 3. *c*)? Does it ever stand alone? What kind of a question is asked by *ne?*[13] The government of *te?* Why is the verb by which it is governed removed to the end of the sentence, and so far from the case it governs? If this is done for the sake of emphasis, how does such an arrangement promote emphasis?[14] Root of *nocturnus?* What is the remainder of it? To what part of speech is it here equivalent (205, R. 15)? Composition of *praesidium?* Literal meaning? What was the *Palatium?* What was the situation and character of this hill? Why was the guard upon the Palatine now, rather than on any other hill?[15] What English word derived from *Palatium?* Why is *nihil* repeated in the successive clauses of this sentence? What is the figure by which such a repetition is designated (324, 13)? Derivation of *urbis?* Why should it be derived from *orbs?* Were the cities in a circular form?[16] Difference between *timor* and *metus?* To what is *timor* opposed? Primary meaning of the word from which *vigiliae* is derived? By what authority were watches posted throughout the city?[17] Was there any stand-

populi, nihil concursus bonorum omnium, nihil hic munitissimus habendi senatus locus, nihil

ing police in the time of the republic?[18] Where was this oration delivered? At the foot of what hill did that temple stand?[19] Composition of *concursus*? The first and second root of the word from which it comes has two *r*'s, why not the third? What English word from it? Meaning? Does it mean merely a running together, or is there the idea of trembling or anxiety connected with it here? What connection between the positive *bonus* and its comparative and superlative? Any in form? Do the comparative and superlative come from *bonus* as a root, or merely supply its defective parts? Who are meant by *bonorum*? Does the word have reference to moral qualities, or does it simply denote patriots, the friends of the state? Are *bonorum* and *omnium* of the same Dec.? That of each? Why *hic* and not *ille*? Derivation of *munitissimus*? What place is meant by *hic locus*?[20] Why was that place said to be *munitissimus*? Was it merely because the Palatine hill, at the foot of which was the temple of Jupiter Stator, was fortified, or because that, in addition to this, Cicero had posted a force around the temple? Is *habendi* a gerund or gerundive? How can this be determined? What would be the form of *senatus* if *habendi* were a gerund? Can there be any doubt, then, whether *habendi* is a gerund or gerundive. Has *senatus* any other form in the Gen. (89, R. 2)? Derivation of *senatus*? Why? What was the senatorial age at this time? How low was it at a later period, in the time of Augustus? What kind of a noun is *locus* (34, R. 2)?

horum ora vultusque moverunt? Patere tua consilia non sentis? Constrictam jam horum

Peculiarity in the Pl.? Different signification of the two forms (92, I. 2)? Difference between *ora* and *vultus*? Derivation of *vultus*? How is it allied to *volo* in meaning? What is the *que* appended to *vultus*? Does it ever stand alone? How does it differ from *et* (198, R. *a*)? Is the *o* in *moverunt* long or short? How is it in the Pres.? By what principle long in the Perf. (284, Exc. 1)? What other form of the third Pers. Pl. Perf. Indic. Act. besides the one here given? Which is used by the best prose writers? Does the form in *-ere* for *-erunt* occur in Cicero?[21] Is *moverunt* Perf. definite or indefinite? Anything to determine this but the connection? The *e* in *pateo* is short, how long in *patēre*?[22] Upon what does *patere* depend? What class of verbs take an Inf. with a subject Acc. (272)? What is the subject Acc. here? Would *vestra* answer here for *tua*? Why not? What is the force of a question introduced by *non*?[23] How was Catiline to see that his purposes were comprehended? By the *praesidium Palatii, urbis vigiliae*, etc.? The *i* in *sentio* is short; is it long or short in *sentis*? How made long?[24] Which conjugation is *sentio*? Is it so in the second and third roots? Which conjugation does it follow in these roots? What becomes of the *t* in the same roots? What occasions the dropping of it? Why is not the subject of *sentis* expressed? Can it be omitted in English? Why not? Force of *con* in *constrictam*? Why does the *n* in the first root disappear in the third? Is it like the *n* in *sino*, etc., dropped

omnium conscientia teneri conjurationem tuam

because it does not belong to the root, or to prevent the accumulation of three consonants? How can it be determined whether the *n* of this word belongs to the root? Is the *n* found in the second root? Does that determine the matter? Is the *n* in *sino* found in the second root as in that of *constringo?* Are the two cases parallel then? By what principle does the *g* in *constringo* become *c* in *constrictam?*[25] *Constrictam* being a Perf. Pass. Part. has the general meaning of *having been bound;* by what usage of the language, then, can it be translated *bound*, or *being bound*, not expressing past time? What idea or relation accompanies the Perf. definite besides that of a past act?[26] Does *constrictam* here denote the past act, or the present state and condition? Does the state or condition sufficiently imply the past act? From what is the metaphor in *constrictam* drawn?[27] What is meant by the metaphorical use of a word (324, 1, *a*)? In what condition is the conspiracy represented by the word *constrictam?* By what means is it *constrictam teneri?* Anything beyond the fact that it is fully understood? What word then describes the means by which its power is checked? In what case is *conscientia?* By what principle? What word is defined or restricted by it? By what word is *conscientia* restricted? What word defines *horum* more fully? Difference between *conscientia* and *scientia?* Does *conscientia* imply that the knowledge belongs to more than one person, and is shared with others? What part of the word implies the sharing of the knowledge? Does *scientia* necessarily imply this? Composition

non vides? Quid proxima, quid superiore nocte egeris, ubi fueris, quos convocaveris, quid con-

of *conjurationem*? Etymological meaning? How has it acquired a bad sense? Is its position more or less emphatic than if it stood with *constrictam*? How more? Does the mere suspense in which the mind is kept as to the word to which *constrictam*, etc., belongs, till *conjurationem* is pronounced or seen, increase the emphasis of the expression? Why *non* here rather than *nonne*?[28] How does *video* compare in signification with *cerno*, *specto*, etc.? What becomes of *d* in the third root of *video*? Why? Is the *e* in *vides* long or short? Why?[29] Why *quid* rather than *quod*? What is the positive of *proxima*? How is the superlative *proximus* obtained? How the *x*? What positive must be assumed to account for the superlative?[30] What night is meant by *proxima nocte*? May *proximus* denote either what is past or future? Which here? If the oration was delivered on the 8th, *proxima nocte* would be the night of what day? Two forms of the superlative of *superior*? How is the form *summus* obtained from *supremus*?[31] Stem of *nocte*? Nom. how formed from the stem? What rejects the *t* from the Nom.? What is that *s*? Construction of *nocte*? Is it proper to say that it is governed by anything? What night is referred to by *superiore nocte*? What was done on that night? At whose house was the meeting held (see chap. 4)? From what does *egeris* come? By what principle is *a* in *ago* changed into *e* in the Perfect? Is the *e* long or short? How made so? What Greek analogy explains the change from *a* to *e*, as well as

silii ceperis, quem nostrum ignorare arbitraris?

the quantity of the *e*?[32] Why is *egeris* in the subjunctive? Are such subjunctives to be translated into English by corresponding subjunctives? What kind of propositions are *quid egeris, ubi fueris, quos convocaveris, quid consilii ceperis*? What is meant by a substantive proposition or clause? In what case are these substantive propositions or clauses, and by what governed? *Ubi* being a conjunctive adverb, what does it connect? What connection has *fueris* with *sum*? Any in form? From what obsolete word is *fueris* derived (154, R. 2)? Any other parts of that word in use besides *fui* and its derivatives (154, R. 3)? From what does *quos* come, *quis* or *qui*? How determined? In *convocaveris* how much is verb-root? What is the last *v*? The *e* following it? Construction of *consilii* (212, R. 3)? Have nouns in *-ius* and *-ium* any other form of the Gen. besides that in *-ii* (52)?[33] Construction of *quem*? By what principle does the Acc. with the Inf. occur here (272)? What is the word here on which the Inf. depends? What is its subject? Full form instead of *nostrum* (133, 3)? Government of (212, R. 2)? Could the Gen. Pl. *nostri* be substituted for *nostrum* here? Why not (212, R. 2, N. 2)? Composition of *ignorare*? What word does the *i* represent (196, 7)? Why is *n* dropped? Would the three consonants *ngn* be euphonic? Whence comes the *g*? Is it retained except in compounds? Primary meaning of *arbitraris*? What kind of a verb? Why called deponent? Construction of *tempora* and *mores* (238, 2)? Stem of *mores*? Why *mos* then in the Nom.?[34] What leads the

O tempora! O mores! Senatus haec intelligit; consul videt: hic tamen vivit. Vivit? Immo

speaker to break out in such an exclamation? Is it that Catiline's plans are so fully comprehended, and yet nothing is done to defeat them? How can the spirit and force of *O tempora! O mores!* be expressed in English? To what does *haec* refer? Composition of *intelligit*? How is the first *l* explained? What becomes of the *g* in the third root? On what principle? What is the figure called by which the connective is omitted between *intelligit* and *videt* [323, 1, (1)]? What is the object of omitting the connective?[35] Why does Cicero say *consul* and not *consules*? Who was the other consul? Had he shown any sympathy with the conspiracy? Would he be likely to coöperate heartily with Cicero in defeating the conspiracy? What does the orator mean by saying *senatus haec intelligit . : . . hic tamen vivit*? What inconsistency is there in these two things? *Tamen* is usually the correlative of a concessive conjunction, as *etsi*, *quanquam*, etc.; but no such conjunction being here expressed, to what concessive expression is *tamen* correlative? What becomes of the second *v* of *vivit* in the second and third roots?[36] Why is *vivit* repeated? Is it for the ordinary emphasis that comes from repeating a word, or is it a question designed to correct a previous statement by introducing something stronger than that which precedes? Is *immo* a negative or affirmative adverb? How may its force be expressed (191, R. 3, near end)? What influence has *vero* upon it?[37] What relation does the clause introduced by *immo* bear to what precedes,—is it stronger or

vero etiam in senatum venit: fit publici consilii particeps: notat et designat oculis ad caedem unumquemque nostrum. Nos autem, viri

weaker? Does the force of *etiam* fall upon *immo* or *venit?* Is the *e* in *venit* long or short? Which in the Perf.? Is the form of the third Pers. Sing. Perf. the same as that of the Pres.? What right had Catiline to come into the senate? Would his former office of Praetor entitle him to this? *Fit* is the passive of what active verb? What is referred to by the *publici consilii*, and what is the force of the statement?[38] Construction of *consilii* (213, R. 1, 3)? Composition of *particeps?* From what is the metaphor drawn in the expression *notat et designat ad caedem?* What is gained to the discourse in this allusion to the priest selecting out his victims for sacrifice? Does it make upon the mind a deeper and more revolting impression of Catiline's bloody purpose? *Notat* and *designat* express one general idea with oratorical fulness, but which denotes the prior act "to put a mark upon," and which "to appoint?" Can the order of the words be changed so as to read *designat et notat?* Why could not *oculis* be omitted? Does he put any actual mark upon them, or simply mark them out in his mind? If *oculis* were omitted, then, would the metaphorical meaning of *notat* as readily present itself? What does *ad* show the relation between? Derivation of *caedem?* Primary meaning? Why not *quemque* without the prefix *unum?* What difference of meaning does *unum* give to *quemque?* Which particularizes more, the simple or the compound? The full force given in English? Why *nos*

fortes, satisfacere reipublicae videmur, si istius furorem ac tela vitemus. Ad mortem te, Catilina, duci jussu consulis jampridem oportebat;

expressed? When are the nominatives of the first and second persons expressed (209, R. 1, *b*)? Why may they not be omitted in English as well as in Latin? What two adversative conjunctions are stronger than *autem?*[39] What place does *autem* occupy in a sentence? What is meant by *viri fortes?* Are the words to be taken in their proper sense? What is the figure called, by which they are here used out of their usual sense (324, 4)? Why did not the orator say *viri imbelles,* using the words in their proper sense? Meaning of *satisfacere* here? What two declensions in *reipublicae?* Construction? Difference of meaning between *si* with the indicative and subjunctive? The appropriateness of *istius* here? Would *hujus* have been as appropriate? Why not? When is *ac* and when *atque* used (198, II. R. *b*)? Would *et* have the same force here as *ac?* Difference between them (198, II, R. *a* and *b*)? Does *tela* denote offensive or defensive weapons? How comparing with *arma?* Is the whole sentence ending with *vitemus* ironical? What does *ad* show the relation between? Why does *ad mortem* stand at the beginning of the sentence? Is the result, or process more prominently in the mind? Why *ad mortem duci,* and not *interfici?* Which is the more forcible expression? Upon what does *duci* depend (271)? Derivation of *jussu?* By what principle two *s*'s? Whence comes the final *u?* Why *jussu consulis* and not *jussu meo?* Does the latter expression in form

in te conferri pestem istam, quam tu in nos

convey any idea of authority? Had the consul a right to put a citizen to death by his own command merely? What was necessary to authorize him to do such an act? Had such authority been given him in this case (see last part of the chapter)? What is the force of *oportebat* in the Impf.? Does it imply that the act was performed at the time when it should have been? Does it imply that the obligation to perform it still exists? Is the time for doing it yet past? Would the Perf. or Plupf. indicate that the act was performed when it should have been? But would either of these tenses imply that the time for doing the act still existed?[40] What kind of a verb is *oportebat?* What is an impersonal verb? But do impersonal verbs ever take a subject? What is the subject of *oportebat* here (269, R. 2)? Is *te* before *conferri* in the Acc. or Abl.? How determined? By what principle has the Pass. Inf. of *confero* two *r*'s?[41] Any other form of *fero* in which *r* is doubled for the same reason? Why *istam* and not *illam?* What two things determine the form of *quam?* Its gender and number are determined by what? Its case by what? Why *tu* expressed? What is noticeable in regard to the position of *tu* and *nos?* When two pronouns occur in the same sentence, how are they usually placed? What is the usual position of *omnis* in relation to the pronoun with which it agrees?[42] Is *machinaris* to be translated into English by a present or a past tense? What warrants or requires this?[43] Does *jamdiu* with the present tense denote that the action has been wholly performed in the past, or that it

omnes jamdiu machinaris. An vero vir amplissimus, P. Scipio, pontifex maximus, Ti.

has been going on in the past and is still in progress in the present? Is *machinaris* particularly appropriate here? Why? What is its precise meaning? Does *an* strictly belong to a single or double question (198, 11, R. *a*)? Is the question double here? *An*, often strengthened by *vero*, is frequently used when the argument proceeds from the less to the greater, *i. e.*, when the second member of the sentence is stronger than the first (can A do something, but cannot B; or if A can, cannot B), — is this the case here, and how shown? Which is the weaker member here? Which the stronger? In what relation does the clause *an vero* ——— *interfecit* stand to *Catilinam* ——— *perferemus*, — coördinate or subordinate? What is gained by making it coördinate, instead of introducing it by the conditional conjunction *si*? Is the contrast, as it is now written, more or less emphatic than if introduced by *si*? If, in translating the sentence into English we use *if* with the first member (the more natural mode of translating), is that member made coördinate or subordinate? In the sentence commencing with *an* and ending with *perferemus*, there are four points of contrast, — what are they? *Scipio* a private man is contrasted with whom? *Gracchus* with whom? A slight attempt against the state with what? The Roman republic with what?[44] Rule for the position of *amplissimus* with reference to *vir*?[45] What does the P. before *Scipio* stand for? What is such a name called? Was that name usually written in full, or only indicated by an initial

Gracchum mediocriter labefactantem statum reipublicae privatus interfecit; Catilinam orbem terrae caede atque incendiis vastare cupientem, nos consules perferemus? Nam illa

(279, 9, *b*)? Derivation of *pontifex?* Would *maximus pontifex* be admissible?[46] Origin of *x* in *maximus?* What was Gracchus endeavoring to accomplish, that he was put to death? Why is his prenomen written *Ti* and not T. merely? What is gained in this sentence by separating *Gracchum* and *Catilinam* so far from their verbs?[47] Derivation of *mediocriter?* Is it often compared? Why not? Composition of *labefactantem?* What kind of a verb is *labefacto?* Literal meaning of? Does *mediocriter labefactantem* fully and truthfully indicate the efforts and aims of *Gracchus?*[48] *Statum,* from what root of what verb? With what does *privatus* agree? Why separated so far from its noun? How does *interficere* differ from *occidere, jugulare, obtruncare, trucidare?* Composition of *interfecit?* Why does Catiline stand first in its clause? Why *orbem terrae,* and not simply *terram?* Composition of *incendiis?* Primary meaning of *candeo?* *Atque,* how comparing with *et?* *Vastare* how with *populari, diripere?* Difference between *cupere* and *velle, optare,* etc.? Peculiarity in the second and third roots of *cupere?* How can *privatus* be reconciled with *pontifex?* Was it true that Catiline was endeavoring to destroy the whole world? How is the expression to be understood then (324, 5)? Why is *consules* used here, — why not *nos* without it sufficient? What is the meaning of *nam* here? Does it express the cause or reason of anything which precedes,

nimis antiqua praetereo, quod C. Servilius Ahala Sp. Maelium, novis rebus studentem,

or is it merely a transition particle, *but?*[49] Difference between *nam* and *enim* (198, 7, R. *a*)? To what does *illa* refer, — to what precedes or follows? Why neuter? Its force or meaning here (207, R. 24)? How is the *d* in the Nom. and Acc. neuter Sing. to be explained?[50] Any other pronoun which has the same endings in these cases? What does *nimis* qualify? What effect has it on *antiqua?* How does *antiquus* differ from *vetus?* Were the events referred to in this sentence prior or subsequent to those mentioned in the previous one? How much? What two forms has *praetereo* in the perfect? How does the form in *ii* come? The orator says he passes over the well-known remote events, and at the same time mentions them; how is this consistent? Does he mean that he will not allude to them at all, or that he will not treat them in full? What connection has the sentence commencing *nam illa* with the orator's subject? Does it make the remissness in punishing Catiline more or less conspicuous? What is the office of *quod?*[51] Which of the names does Servilius denote? Which Ahala? Who was Ahala? For what did he put Maelius to death? Derivation of *novis?* Origin of the *v* in it? Declension of *rebus?* The fourth and fifth declensions are merely modifications of what other Dec.? Case of *rebus?* By what principle? What different cases does *studeo* govern? Gender of *manu?* According to rule or exception? Why *sua* and not *ejus?* Why expressed at all here (207, R. 36, *c*)? Would it not be understood to be by his hand if

manu sua occidit. Fuit, fuit ista quondam in hac republica virtus, ut viri fortes acrioribus suppliciis civem perniciosum quam acerbissi-

sua were omitted? Composition of *occidit?* Why two *c*'s? Why *fuit* at the beginning of the sentence? Why repeated? Meaning of *ista* here? Composition of *quondam?* Is *e* in *republica* long or short? How comes it so? Derivation of *virtus?* Does it mean virtue here? What? Its primary meaning? Why is it placed last in its clause? How does its present position give it emphasis? Would *homines* answer as well as *viri* here? Difference between them? Derivation of *fortes?* How is *viri fortes* here used? What is gained by this ironical use? Primary meaning of *acrioribus?* Connection between the primary meaning and the one here? How is its superlative formed? Composition of *suppliciis?* How does it have such different meanings as those of *prayer* and *punishment?* Its construction? With what word is *civem* contrasted? Composition of *perniciosum?* Meaning of each of its component parts? Force of adjectives ending in *osus?* From what does *quam* come? Primary meaning of *hostis?* How different from *inimicus?* From what is *acerbissimum* formed? What termination is added? Composition of *coercerent?* Force of the preposition? How does the *e* after *o* originate?[52] Why the subjunctive? What is the *n* before *t?* If it is removed, in what number and person will the verb be? What is noticeable in the change of position of *acerbissimum* and *hostem* as compared with *civem perniciosum?* Why not *hostem acerbissimum*, as well as *civem perniciosum?* What advan-

mum hostem coercerent. Habemus senatus consultum in te, Catilina, vehemens et grave: non deest reipublicae consilium neque auctoritas hujus ordinis: nos, nos, dico aperte, consules desumus.

tage in this change?[53] What was a *senatus consultum?* When was the one here referred to passed?[54] What was the formula, or words used?[55] With what power did it clothe the consuls? Is *te* in the Acc. or the Abl.? Why are *vehemens* and *grave* removed from the substantive to which they belong? Is the composition of *vehemens* definitely determined? Has *grave* its primary sense here? Is *reipublicae* in the Gen. or Dat.? How would it be constructed if it were in the Dat.? Would the meaning resulting from such a construction be inappropriate here? If taken as a Gen., is it a subjective or objective Gen.? What would *reipublicae consilium* mean as a subjective Gen.? What as an objective Gen.? What is meant by a subjective Gen. (211, R. 2)? Does the Gen. *ordinis* give any intimation of the case of *reipublicae?* Difference between *consilium* and *concilium?* Derivation of *auctoritas?* Stem? What occasions the dropping of the final *t?* What body is meant by *hujus ordinis?* Nom. of *ordinis?* Stem? How from the stem is the Nom. formed? Derivation of *aperte?* Is there anything noticeable in *deest* being at the beginning of this sentence, and *desumus* at the end? Why are *consules* and *desumus* brought together?

VIRGIL.

QUESTIONS ON THE FIRST THIRTY-THREE LINES OF THE AENEID.

WHEN was Virgil born? Where? Was it in Italy or Gaul at that time? At what time was his birthplace first included in Italy? What was that part of the country called before? Who were the consuls at Rome the year he was born? Was he older or younger than Augustus? How much? How much older than Horace? Was he a contemporary of Cicero? Older or younger? In what two places in northern Italy was he educated? In what place in southern Italy is he said to have studied? Did he receive any part of his education at Rome? What was the occasion of his losing his hereditary estate? What connection had he with Asinius Pollio? What was the ground of attachment existing between them? To what distinguished patron of literature at Rome did Pollio introduce him? Through whom did he become acquainted with Augustus? Did Augustus show him any favors besides encouraging him in his literary pursuits? Were any of his works composed at Naples? Was there probably any cause of his residence there besides the attractiveness of the place? Had he a vigorous constitution? May his health, then, have been the cause of his seeking a milder climate than was to be found in the mountainous region of his native place? Did he visit any foreign country? What? Did he travel there extensively? When and where did he die? How happened he to be at Brundusium? Where was he buried? Is the spot where he was buried now known with certainty?[1]

Why is this poem called the *Aeneid?* Who is the hero? Is Aeneas a mythical or historical person in the *Aeneid?*[2] Is it certain that he ever came to Italy? May Virgil have intended to describe the character and achievements of some other person under the name of Aeneas? How long was Virgil in writing this poem? Was it finished at the time of his death, as he intended it should be? How many years after the fall of Troy does the scene open? Where are Aeneas and the Trojans at the opening of the first book? Is the first book the first in the order of time? Which is first in the order of time? Second? Third? What is gained by this change in the chronological order of the first book? Is the interest of the reader greater or less by being hurried at once into the subject, and then having the historical detail presented afterwards by persons with whose characters he has already become interested? Is there any similar change of chronological order in the Paradise Lost? Which book of that poem is first chronologically? What kind of a poem is the Aeneid? What is meant by an Epic poem? Could it also be called an Heroic poem? On what ground could this and similar poems be so called? What are the first seven lines? What do they contain?[3]

ARMA virumque cano, Trojae qui primus ab oris

Why do *arma* and *virum* stand the first words in the poem? Different senses of *arma?* Ever used in Sing.? Is *arma* and *virum* a case of Hendyadis [323, 2, (3)], signifying the warlike achievements of the hero? If not, what is the meaning of each? Which denotes the warlike achievements, and which the personal adventures? Construction of these accusatives? Are they the objects of *cano* in any such sense as when we say, *I sing a song*, or are they a kind of cognate Acc., — *I sing the song of the arms and the hero?* (Compare "I sing the sofa.") Why *cano, i. e.*, in what sense does he sing?[4] Peculiarity of *cano* in the second root? By what principle is the vowel of the reduplication *e?*[5] *Trojae* where? Construction? What influence has it on *oris?* Which was the earlier and Greek name, *Troja* or *Ilium?* Was *Pergamus* the same as *Troja?* How different? In what country was Troy situated? Near what sea? Is the site now known? What word determines three features of *qui?* What are they? What two features of what word does *qui* determine? What are they? The positive of *primus?* From what contracted? Why is the *i* long? When is *prior* and when *primus* to be used? Was Aeneas the first who came from Troy to Italy? Did not Antenor come before (see line 242 seq.)? How are these statements to be reconciled? To what part of Italy did Antenor come? Would *primum* have the same meaning as *primus* here? Difference? Why *ab* and not *a* here? Between what does *ab* show the relation, *oris* and *profugus*, or *oris* and *venit*, or both? Difference between *oris* and *litora?*

Italiam, fato profugus, Laviniaque venit

How many feet in a line here? From the number of feet in a line, what is the verse called? What is the predominant foot in hexameter verse? Why not all the feet dactyls? Would an unbroken succession of dactyls be as harmonious as a variety in the measure? What is the other foot besides the dactyl here? Derivation of the word *spondee?* Derivation of *dactyl?*[6] What is the greatest number of syllables in an hexameter line? The least?[7] How disposed of in each case? What is a caesura? Design of it? Where is the caesura of the verse, or caesural pause in the first line? Is it the masculine or feminine caesura (310, N. 1)? What is meant by a masculine caesura? What by a feminine? Is the place of the caesural pause fixed in hexameter verse (309, R. 3)? What is the most approved place for the caesural pause in epic poetry (310, 4)? By what principle is *a* in *cano* short? What is meant when it is said to be short by authority, or by the authority of the poets? Does not the authority or usage of the poets determine the quantity of all vowels? Is there not just the same authority for the final *a* of *arma* being short, as for *a* in *cano?* Why, then, is the latter said to be short by authority, but the former by rule (final *a* in words declined is short)?[8]

Construction of *Italiam?* Is it usual to omit the preposition with the names of countries (237, R. 5, *c*)? Would a good prose writer omit or use the preposition here? Would *in Romam venit* be good Latin? Would *in Hispaniam venit?* What is the difference in the two cases that makes

Litora; multum ille et terris jactatus et alto,

in requisite in one and not in the other? By what principle is the first *i* in *Italiam*, which is usually short, long here?[9] Had the peninsula subsequently known as *Italia*, in earlier times any name which designated the whole? To what different portions was the term *Italia* applied at different periods? How early did the name embrace the whole peninsula? Derivation of *fato?* Why *a* long? Why in Abl.? Why used at all? Without it, would it be clear, at this point, whether he was a mere adventurer, banished for his misdeeds, or an exile by the appointment of the gods? Derivation of *profugus?* Is it to be taken in a good or bad sense: a fugitive or an exile? What feeling for the hero is the word adapted to produce? Where was *Lavinium?* Why so named? What relation does *Lavinia litora* bear to *Italiam?* Could *Lavinia litora* change place with *Italiam*, so as to stand before it? Why not? Do we usually place the general or specific first? If *Lavinium* was not upon the sea-coast, how can the poet say *Lavinia litora?* Is the *que* appended to *Lavinia* a connective, "and," or an expletive, "even"? Were there any *Lavinia litora* when Aeneas came there? By what figure, then, does he speak of them as existing at that time? What figure in the scanning of *Laviniaque* (306, 1)? Does the form of *venit* determine whether it is Pres. or Perf.? What is the quantity of the *e* when *venit* is Pres.? What when it is Perf. (284, Exc. 1)? In what tense, then, is it here? In prose is there any means of determining the tense, except by the connection? As *litora* is

Vi superum, saevae memorem Junonis ob iram;

neither the name of a town or a country, by what principle is it in the Acc.? Is *Lavinia litora*, so far as relates to construction, different from what *Lavinium* would have been in its place? How, then, would *Lavinium* have been constructed? Is the *o* in *litora* short by rule or exception? What is the rule and what the exception? What becomes of the *um* of *multum* in scanning? What is the figure called by which it is elided (305, 2)? By what figure is the *e* of *ille* elided (305, 1)? What Greek pronoun corresponds to *ille?* Has *ille* here its full pronomial force, or does it merely recall or resume the subject, giving a more lively expression? Force of *et* before *terris?* Could it be omitted without essentially changing the expression? Precisely what would be lost by its omission?[10] With what is this *et* correlative, or with what does it correspond? Why is *terris* plural? Were his calamities experienced in one land or several? Why Abl.? In good prose is the preposition more commonly expressed or omitted with ablatives of place (254, R. 3)? What kind of a verb is *jacto,* from which *jactatus* comes? What does such a verb imply (187, II. 1)? Of which conjugation are frequentatives? What is the simple verb from which *jacto* is formed? From what part of that verb? Does *jactatus* apply equally to *terris* and *alto?* To which does it apply in its appropriate sense? What is the figure by which it is connected with both, when it properly belongs to but one [323, 1, (2)]? Is *est* to be understood with *jactatus* and *passus,* or are these pure participles merely? Is *alto* strictly an

Multa quoque et bello passus, dum conderet urbem,

adjective or a substantive? Any English word similarly used? What is the primary meaning of *altus*, from which it has the signification of both *high* and *deep?* Where is the caesural pause in the third line? From what Greek word does *vi* come? Origin of the *v?* Is *vis* actually defective in any case?[11] What case is used very rarely? What relation does the Abl. *vi* express? By what principle in the Abl.? Who are meant by the plural *superum*, —any one but Juno? What relation does *superum* sustain to *vi?* Full form of *superum?* What are the two forms of the superlative of this word? How is the shorter form, *summus*, obtained from the other form?[12] Difference between *supremus* and *summus?* To what word is *supremus* opposed? To what *summus?* Which is commonly used in prose? With reference to what is Juno called *saevae;* or is this epithet applied to her as a general characteristic? *Memorem* properly belongs only to persons, how then is *iram* to be considered? Who was Juno? From what root, and how, is the Nom. formed?[13] Whence comes the *n* in the oblique cases? What were the grounds of Juno's anger here referred to (see lines 25—28)? The relations expressed by *vi superum* and *ob iram* respectively, *i.e.*, which is instrument and which cause? Has MULTA *passus* the same signification as MULTUM *passus* would have? *Quoque* means *moreover* in addition to what? What particle would generally be used, in good prose, instead of *et*, after *quoque?*[14] Upon what word does the force

Inferretque deos Latio: genus unde Latinum,
Albanique patres, atque altae moenia Romae.

of *et* fall? Is *bello* Abl. of *means* or *time*? Its derivation? How does the *d* become *b*? By what principle two *s*'s in *passus*? What would be its form before assimilation? Does *dum* here signify *until* or *while*? Why followed by the subjunctive?[15] Composition of *conderet*? Of which conjugation is the simple? The compound? Primary meaning of *conderet*? Peculiarity in the second root? Derivation of *urbem*? What connection between it and *orbis*? How do the two *r*'s come together in *inferret*? What letter is syncopated? What relation does the second root bear to the first? How is the third root, *latum*, derived from the second?[16] Is *deos* here in its usual sense, or is it equivalent to *penates*? What occasion for adverting to the idea contained in *inferret deos* at all? In the view of a Roman, would religion be indispensably connected with the founding of a flourishing city? Is the Dat. *Latio* the usual construction in such cases? What is more common (225, IV. and R. 2)? What and where was *Latium*? From what was the name probably derived? Were the names of places more frequently derived from the names of the people, or the people from the places?[17] Stem of *genus*? To what does *unde* refer, and what is its meaning? If it is translated *from this circumstance*, what is the meaning of this expression? How are the Alban fathers and the walls of Rome *unde*? Which way was *Alba* from *Lavinium*? Rome from *Alba*? Why called *Alba*? Why *Longa*? Is the actual site of *Alba* known beyond a doubt?

Musa, mihi causas memora, quo numine laeso,

In what sense is *patres* here used? Is it that of being the founders of *Alba*, or the *nobles*, for the purpose of giving dignity to the place? Construction of *genus*, *patres*, etc.? Why is *Romae* called *altae?* On how many hills was it built? Why built on hills? Derivation of *moenia?* How differing from *muri* and *parietes?* Difference between *atque* and *et?* When was Rome founded? Situation? On the sea? How far from? On what river? On which bank?

What are the next four lines called? Derivation of *Musa?* Does ου in Greek uniformly become *u* in Latin? Why *u* in *musa* long? How many Muses? What determined the character of the *Muse* to be invoked? In the Georgics Virgil invokes Ceres, Pan, Minerva, Bacchus, Pales, Maecenas, etc.; why the Muse here? Who was the Muse of epic poetry? Does *mihi* come from *ego* as its root? What part of *mihi* is root, and what termination?[18] Are the singular and plural formed from the same root? What other forms for Dat. Sing. besides *mihi* (133, R. 1)? Is the quantity of the final *i* uniform? How was the word *causa* written in Cicero's time, and before?[19] Derivation of *memora?* Has it its primary or secondary sense? Its direct and indirect object? Why is the *a* long? Is *quo* a pronoun or adverb? With what agreeing? Derivation of *numine?* How much is verb root? What is the remainder? Nom.? Stem? Why is the *i* of the stem (*nomin*) changed to *e* in the Nom.? Which has the more open, and which the closer sound? Is the close sound of

Quidve dolens regina deum tot volvere casus

i felt in the oblique cases as it would be in the Nom.? What rules determine the quantity of the vowels of *numine?* Meaning here? Construction? The thwarting of what purpose (*numine*) or object is referred to? What place was Juno intending to make the mistress of the world? What influences were now at work to prevent this? Pres. of *laeso?* What becomes of *d* in the second and third roots? What letter of these roots rejects the *d?* How much of *laeso* is root? What is the remainder? Construction of *quid* (232, 1 and N. 1)? But how has *quid* a signification kindred to that of *dolens?*[20] *Ve* formed from what? And *vel* from what? Does *ve* ever stand alone? What is it called then? How differing from *aut* and *vel* (198, 2, R. *b.*)? Toward whom was the resentment denoted by *dolens* cherished? Why towards Paris and Ganymede? Who is meant by *regina deum?* What is this figure called [323, 2 (4)]? Is the *e* in *regina* long by rule or authority? Rule for the quantity of *i?* What is the correlative of *tot?* Has it any correlative here expressed? Is any to be supplied? Is it used here, then, to denote a definite or indefinite number? How is it declined? Third root of *volvere?* What becomes of the second *v?* When does such a change take place?[21] What is the pertinence of the word *volvere* here? Does it signify simply to *endure* or *suffer* calamities, or does it imply a constant succession, a round or interminable series of them? Would good prose put *volvere* in the Inf., as here, or in the Subj.? Upon what does it depend? From which root

Insignem pietate virum, tot adire labores,
Impulerit. Tantaene animis coelestibus irae!

of what verb does *casus* come? What has occasioned the dropping of the *d* of the verb? Is the final syllable long or short? From what is that syllable a contraction (89, R. 1)? Is the word in itself taken in a good or a bad sense, or both? Which is predominant? In which here? Composition of *insignem?* Primary meaning? Derivation of *pietate?* What kind of a noun (26, 5)? What is meant when Aeneas is said to be *insignem pietate?* Does it signify merely what we mean by *piety*, or *devotion to the gods*, or does it imply also *filial devotion, kind and affectionate conduct toward others?* How from *adeo* is the Inf. *adire* formed? When is the initial letter of *eo i*, and when *e?* What other construction does *adire* take besides the naked Acc.? Composition of *impulerit?* Whence comes the *m?* When in composition letters of a different order (*i. e.*, requiring different organs to pronounce them) come together, what is to be done? The *p* in this word is a labial, and the *n* of the preposition *in* is a dental; this dental must, then, be changed into a letter of what order? Is *m*, then, of the same order as *p?* What organs are used in pronouncing each? Does the second *l* of *pello* belong to the root, or is it a strengthening letter of the Pres.? How can this be shown? If it belonged to the root, would it or would it not be retained in the second root? Of what vowel of the Pres. of this word is *u* the representative in the second and third roots? When is *e* changed into *u?*[22] Derivation of *tantae?* Why is the *m* of *tam* changed into

Urbs antiqua fuit, Tyrii tenuere coloni,

n? Is the letter *t* of the termination a dental or a lingual? To what, then, must the *m* be changed? Construction of *animis?* Derivation of *coelestibus?* What connection between heaven and κοῖλον, meaning an *arch?* Is the name derived from the actual form of the heavens, or sky, or from the *apparent* form? Why *irae* plural? Do the poets often use the plural for the sake of emphasis or the metre?[23]

How does *antiqua* differ from *vetus?* Which denotes what existed long ago? Do they both have all the forms of comparison? Why is *antiqua* used at all? Did the antiquity of a city give it more or less celebrity? With reference to whom was the city said to be *antiqua*, Aeneas or Virgil? Was it really built in the time of Aeneas? Does *fuit* here imply that the city was or was not then in existence (Comp. II. 325)? From what noun does *Tyrii* come? Where was old Tyre situated? In what country? Was it upon the mainland or on an island? What is the grammatical object of *tenuere?* Is it expressed or to be supplied? Any other form for the third Pers. Pl. Perf. besides *tenuere?* What form would Cicero use? What tense would the Greek use for it? What is the difference between the Greek Aorist and the Lat. Perf.? What two relations does the Lat. Perf. express? By what two Greek tenses are these relations expressed? In this respect, which language has the advantage in point of definiteness? Derivation of *coloni?* Construction of *Carthago?* Where situated? When, and by whom founded? Stem?

Carthago, Italiam contra Tiberinaque longe
Ostia, dives opum, studiisque asperrima belli;

How from the stem is the Nom. formed? Is anything gained by omitting the name of the city in the first line? What? Does the suspense make the impression of the suppressed word stronger or weaker when it is named? Is the position of *Carthago* at the beginning of the line more or less emphatic, than if it had been in the middle?[24] What is noticeable in the position of *Italiam*, with reference to the word which governs it (279, 10, *f.*)? Is this usual in prose? What relation does *Italiam* sustain to *Tiberina ostia?* What *Tiberina ostia* to *Italiam?* What direction was Carthage from the mouth of the Tiber? What sea between? When was that sea first called the *Mare Mediterraneum?*[25] *Dives*, with what agreeing? What is the comparative, and how formed? How differing from *locuples?* Construction of *opum?* Rule (213, R. 1, 3)? How many cases of the Sing. are in use? What is such a word called (94, 1)? How does the plural differ in meaning from the singular? What does *que* after *studiis* connect? Construction of *studiis* (250)? Is it governed by anything? It shows in what respect what word is taken? Is it, therefore, explanatory of the meaning of *asperrima?* What word is explanatory of *studiis?* Primary meaning of *asperrima?* Has it here its primary or secondary sense? Antecedent of *quam?* By what rule is its antecedent feminine? What is omitted in *fertur* (179)? Construction of *terris?* The office of such ablatives is to complete the comparison; by what word is the comparison begun or

Quam Juno fertur terris magis omnibus unam
Posthabita coluisse Samo : hic illius arma,

introduced here? What is the office of *unam* here? What word does it strengthen, *quam* or *magis?* Is *unus* as an intensive or strengthening word found more frequently with the comparative or superlative?[26] How can its force be expressed here? Could it be translated either by *one* or *alone?* Would *in particular* indicate its force? Is its emphasis increased or diminished by standing at the end of the line?[24] Composition and literal meaning of *posthabita?* Is it here in its primary or secondary sense, denoting a local or mental *putting after?* What determines its gender? Upon what does *coluisse* depend? Rule (271)? What change takes place in the vowel of the stem in the third root? Does *o* often interchange with *u?*[27] Where was *Samos?* In what sea? Why mentioned in this connection at all? Rule for its gender? Construction? When it is said to be in the ablative absolute, what is meant by the term *absolute?* Would the genitive absolute be used to express this in Greek? Why not? What is the difference between the Latin and Greek here, that the same construction would not be used in both?[28] What participle would be used in Greek, instead of the Latin Perf. here? In what case would the Greek participle be, and with what agreeing? In what case would *Samo* be? Is the *o* in *Samo* retained or elided? But does not the retaining of it cause hiatus, the *o* coming before the *i* in *hic?* How is the effect of the hiatus prevented here? In Virgil does the hiatus more commonly occur in the Arsis

Hic currus fuit; hoc regnum dea gentibus esse,
Si qua fata sinant, jam tum tenditque fovetque.

or Thesis?[29] To what does *hic* refer? What was the old ablative form from which it comes?[30] Has the penult *i* in *illius* any other quantity than it has here? In Virgil is it more frequently long or short?[31] What does the poet mean by saying *hic illius arma, hic currus fuit?* To what word is *fuit* conformed? How is *arma* disposed of? To what does *hoc* refer? Why not, then, in the feminine gender (206, 8)? Does the gender of pronouns conform to the words to which they refer, or to those with which they agree? What may this properly be called?[32] Is *hoc* an adjective pronoun here agreeing with *regnum*, or has it a substantive force? Construction? Construction of *regnum?* How is it determined that *regnum* is the predicate Acc. after *esse*, and not the predicate Nom. (210)? What would have been a more natural construction for *regnum* than to be in the Acc. (227, R. 4)? Dat. and Abl. Pl. of *dea?* Why (43, 2)? Have any other words of the first Dec. similar forms? Construction of *gentibus* (227)? What is the other Dat., besides *gentibus?* What would have been that other Dat., if the more usual construction had been followed here? How is the second *s* in *esse* to be explained?[33] Upon what does *esse* depend? What class of words admit the Acc. with the Inf. (272)? Is *qua* in the Nom. Pl., agreeing with *fata* (*if any fates*), or in the Abl.? Is there any way to determine this certainly? What? Could it be determined in prose? How better in poetry? *Si* followed by the Subj. here implies what? That the

Progeniem sed enim Trojano a sanguine duci
Audierat, Tyrias olim quae verteret arces;

fates would permit? That they would not permit? Does it imply anything definitely, or merely express a *supposition*, without determining whether they would or would not permit? Root of *sinant?* What is the first *n?* In what tenses is it retained? What is the last *n?* How are the second and third roots formed? Is the caesura in this line masculine or feminine? What is the office of *jam*, *i. e.*, what word is affected by it, and how? How may *jam tum* be rendered here? What would *even then* denote: that even when she was beginning to build Carthage, and before it had reached its destined influence, she was intending to make it the ruler of the nations? Peculiarity of *tendit* in the second root? Why is *d* rejected in the third root? Primary meaning? What is the figure called by which the two *que*'s are here used [323, 2 (2)]? What is the object of using the two *que*'s?[34] Is the force of each verb increased or diminished by them? How? What becomes of *v* in the third root of *fovet?* Why? Is the idea of *fovet* stronger or weaker than that of *tendit?* Composition of *progeniem?* Does *sed* usually stand the second word in a sentence in prose (279, 3, *a*)? Is the word denoting the contrast introduced by *sed* expressed or understood? What is the purport of that word? What does *enim* express the reason of? What does *a* show the relation between? Stem of *sanguine?* What rejects the *n* of the stem in the Nom.? Any peculiarity in *audierat?* When and how does such contraction occur (162, 7, *a*)? From what Greek letter

Hinc populum late regem belloque superbum
Venturum excidio Libyae: sic volvere Parcas.

does the *y* of *Tyrias* come? What different relations of time does *olim* express? What letter of *verteret* is dropped in the third root? Why? Would the combination *rts* be euphonic? Why might not the *r* or the *s* be dropped as well as the *t*? Would it answer to drop a prominent letter of the root or of the termination? Why *verteret* in the subjunctive (264, 1, *a*)? But is there any demonstrative in the antecedent clause to which *quae* refers? Is such demonstrative often understood? Stem of *arces*? Nom. how formed from it? Why were these *arces* called *Tyrias*? To what does *hinc* refer? In what other way might the idea contained in it have been expressed? Construction of *populum*? What does *late* qualify? But how can an adverb qualify a noun (277, R. 1)? What office, however, does *regem* perform, that of a noun or a participle? Is such a usage admissible in prose? What is the figure by which one part of speech is used for another [323, 3, (*b*), (1)]? Is *bello* Abl. of *respect* or of *cause*? Does it express the cause of *superbum*? But is it war merely that they were to be proud of, or does the *superbum* necessarily imply success, so that the meaning is, *proud of their success in war*? Would *potentem* have been as forcible a word here as *superbum*? Does *superbum* imply *potentem*, and something besides? What is understood with *venturum*? What Inf. is it? From what root is the Fut. Inf. formed? Upon what does *venturum* [*esse*] depend? What is its subject Acc.? Composition of *excidio*? Case? What case is

Id metuens, veterisque memor Saturnia belli,
Prima quod ad Trojam pro caris gesserat Argis:
Necdum etiam causae irarum saevique dolores

Libyae? What rule for two datives with *venturum* (227)? What do the poets often use *Libyae* for? To what does *sic* refer, or how much of what precedes does it cover? On what does *volvere* depend? What is the pertinence of the word here? What letter changes in the third root? Is *Parcas* the subject or the object of *volvere?* Derivation? What connection in meaning has it with *pars* or *partior?* What is the Greek word for *Fates?* Has the Greek word the same signification as the Latin? To what does *id* refer? How is the *d* to be explained?[35] How is the superlative of *veteris* formed? Has the word all the degrees of comparison? Meaning here? What does *que* after *veteris* connect? Is *memor* compared? Who is meant by *Saturnia?* Why so called? Subject of what verb? What is meant by *veteris belli?* How long prior to the time of which the poet is here speaking did the war begin? It cannot mean the *old* or *ancient war*, then; what is the meaning? Does *prima* agree with *Saturnia* or a pronoun understood? Does *prima* mean *formerly*, or *as chief, foremost?* Is *quod* here in the position it would have in prose? In what part of its clause does it stand in prose?[36] What letter of the stem does the first *s* in *gesserat* represent? Why changed? What is the second *s?* Nom. Sing. of *Argis?* How declined? Where was Argos? Does it mean here nothing but the city? What is its meaning? The sentence commencing with *nec* is parenthetic; where

Exciderant animo: manet alta mente repostum
Judicium Paridis spretaeque injuria formae,
Et genus invisum, et rapti Ganymedis honores:

does the parenthesis end? What is *nec* here, as often elsewhere, equivalent to (198, II. 1. R. *c*)? Does *etiam* here mean *also*, *likewise*, or *even*? Upon what word does its force fall? What were the *causae irarum*, etc.? Where expressed? What relation, then, do *causae irarum*, etc., sustain to *manet* .... *honores*? Composition of *exciderant*? By what principle does the *a* of *cado* become *i* in composition?[37] Syntax of *animo*? Literal meaning of *exciderant animo*? Subject of *manet*? Why not plural then? What idea is intended to be conveyed by *alta*? Composition of *repostum*? Stem of *pono*? How from the stem *pos* is *pono* formed? What is the *n*? What letter does it reject? In what roots does that letter reappear? Why? What letter is syncopated in *repostum*? What was the *judicium Paridis*? Who was Paris? Stem of the word? Nom.? Why the *d* rejected? From what verb does *spretae* come? What has become of the *n* of the Pres.? What change has taken place in the position of the *r*? What is meant by *metathesis* (322, 9)? From what theme, then, is *spretae* formed?[38] What relation does *spretae injuria formae* sustain to *judicium Paridis*? *Formae* from what Greek word? By what change? What race is meant by *genus*? Why were they *invisum*? From whom was the Trojan race descended? Composition of *invisum*? How from *invideo*, which primarily means *to look upon*, or *look intently upon*, does the idea of *hatred* or *envy* come? How

His accensa super, jactatos aequore toto
Troas reliquias Danaum atque immitis Achilli,

do we regard that which we look upon with great interest, and desire to obtain, but cannot? Does *rapti* agree with *Ganymedis* or *honoris?* Will the form of the words or the connection either determine it absolutely? Making it agree with *Ganymedis,* to what fact does it refer? How was Ganymede carried away? Who was he? Why should Juno complain of the honors bestowed upon him? To what does *his* refer? Composition of *accensa?* The first *c*, how explained? What letter is dropped, and why? Incensed by these things in addition to (*super*) what else? Which was the greater ground of her trouble, the circumstances just mentioned, or her fears that her purpose to make Carthage the ruling power among the nations would be defeated by the Trojan colony which was to settle in Italy? What is the simple verb from which the frequentative *jacto* is formed? Derivation of *aequore?* Construction? Could the preposition be omitted in prose if *toto* were joined with *aequore* (254, R. 2, *b*)? *Aequor* how differing from *mare, pontus,* and *pelagus?* Difference between *totus* and *omnis?* Is *Troas* a pure Latin form (86)? Derivation of *reliquias?* What letter of the Pres. is dropped? Does that letter belong to the root of *relinquo?* Will it convey the right idea in English, to translate *reliquias Danium* "the remnants of the Greeks"; or has the Gen. here a subjective force: "those left or spared by the Greeks"? From whom did the *Danai* derive their name? What people of Greece did the name properly designate? Does it in-

Arcebat longe Latio: multosque per annos

clude nothing more than the Argives here, or does it denote the Greeks generally? Why should the *Danai* more than some other class be taken to represent the whole body of Greeks? Was this a powerful or a weak tribe at the time referred to? Full form instead of *Danaum*? Would *et* be as appropriate here as *atque*? Which expresses the idea of "more particularly," "and moreover?" Does *atque* draw more or less attention to Achilles than *et* would? Why should any special attention be drawn to him? How is the first *m* in *immitis* to be explained? What three other forms of the Gen. of Achilles besides *Achilli* (86)? Subject of *arcebat*? Why Impf.? Construction of *Latio* (251)? By what means was she keeping them from *Latium*? What object had she in doing this? What connection between *multos* and its comparative *plus*? Any in form? What is the superlative of *plus*? How does the superlative *plurimus* come from *plus*? What is the stem of *plus*? What is added to the stem, then, to form the superlative? But do not stems ending in *r*, as *veter*, *miser*, etc., add *rimus* to the stem for the superlative? Why not *plurrimus*, then, with two *r*'s? Is the *u* in *plus*, however, long or short? Does the vowel then need to be lengthened by *position*? But is the *e* before *r* in *veter* long or short? Why is *per* expressed here? Would not *annos* be in the Acc. of duration of time without it? Does the poet wish to make the length of time as prominent as possible, or the reverse? Is the length of time more prominent with or without *per*? He says "many years"—how many? Why did he not

Errabant acti fatis maria omnia circum.
Tantae molis erat Romanam condere gentem!

name the number definitely, then? Is the impression more or less forcible by the indefinite mode of expression? The idea of the length of time, then, is here denoted in three different ways — what are they? Does the form of the verb *errabant* also contribute to the same effect? What feature of that form does this? By what principle does the *g* in *ago* become *c* in *acti*?[39] Why *maria omnia*, and not *mare omne*, as all his wanderings were in the *Mediterranean*? What is noticeable about the position of *circum*? Construction of *molis* (211, R. 8. 3)? Is it necessary to suppose that any substantive is omitted here by which *molis* is governed? Does not the Gen. follow *sum* constantly to denote the relations expressed by the rule of the grammar? What is the subject of *erat*? Why *erat* in the Impf.? Does it imply that the difficulty existed at every step in the efforts to establish the nation?

XENOPHON.

QUESTIONS ON THE FIRST CHAPTER OF THE ANABASIS.

WAS Xenophon born at Athens? Where? Why called an Athenian, then? When was he born? Can the time be determined definitely? How much is known of his early life? In what battle did he take part more than twenty years before the Expedition of Cyrus? How does tradition report him to have been saved in that battle? Was there any intimacy between him and Socrates in after life? From whom did he receive his most valuable instruction? Had Socrates any particular place where he instructed his pupils?[1] Through whose influence was Xenophon induced to join the Expedition? From what part of Greece was Proxenus? Why had he come to Athens? Under what circumstances had Xenophon become acquainted with him?[2] In what did Gorgias give instruction? Did Xenophon connect himself with the Expedition for the purpose of taking part in it, or that he might be associated with his friend, and obtain some advantage from Cyrus? At about what age did he join the Expedition? Did he consult any one in regard to going? Whom? What answer did Socrates give him? Did he follow the directions given? How did he deviate from them?

During the Peloponnesian war Cyrus had coöperated with the Peloponnesians against the Athenians — was it consistent, then, for Xenophon, as an Athenian, to join those who had aided the enemies of his country? Did his countrymen look upon his course as treasonable? Did he ever return to Athens after he joined the Expedition? Was there anything to prevent his doing so? What? Did he engage in any other military enterprise after that of Cyrus? Did he fight against his countrymen in any battle? In what? Where did he settle after his military campaigns were over? Who gave him this place?[3] Is it probable that he wrote his works there? Did he continue there the remainder of his life? Where did he probably die? At about what age?

What was the object of the Expedition of Cyrus? Why called Anabasis? To how much of the whole treatise called the *Anabasis* does the term properly belong? What is the remainder properly called? Who was King of Persia at the time the Expedition commenced? How long had he been king? Had Cyrus any claim to the throne in preference to Artaxerxes? Which was the elder son? Was either or both of them born before Darius came to the throne? Had there been any instance in which a younger son had become king, to the exclusion of an elder one? What? Was Xerxes the eldest son born after his father was king? Was this the case with Cyrus? Being the eldest son of *King* Darius, and having the precedent of Xerxes before him, had he any ground to suppose that the kingdom might be given to him? In what year did the Expedition commence? What peculiar facilities were there

ΔΑΡΕΙΟΥ καὶ Παρυσάτιδος γίγνονται παῖδες δύο,

at this time for obtaining Grecian soldiers? What long-protracted war in Greece had just terminated? Were the soldiers who had been engaged in that war now thrown out of employment? Had Cyrus assisted either the Athenians or Lacedemonians in the Peloponnesian war? Which? What advantage would that be to him in obtaining soldiers? Were most of his Grecian mercenaries Athenians or Peloponnesians? Why? In what month did the Expedition start from Ephesus? In what from Sardis?[4] Did either the Grecian or Barbarian force of Cyrus understand the object he had in view? The whole time occupied in the Expedition? What position did Cyrus hold at the time it commenced? At what age had he been appointed satrap?[5] Whom did he succeed? What did his satrapy embrace?[6] Who were the two satraps associated with him? What relation did he sustain to them?[7] Where were the satrapies of the other two? How many years had he held his office before the Expedition? What was his age when it commenced? What was the condition of the Persian Empire at this time, compared with its condition a hundred years previous? What two expeditions had the Persians made in that time into Greece? With what result?

Nom. of Παρυσάτιδος? Stem? How is the stem found in the third declension (32, 1)? What letter rejects δ in the Nom. (8. 7)? How can it reappear in the Gen.?[8] What is the σ that is appended to the stem?[9] Construction of Δαρείου and Παρυσάτιδος (158, 1)? Who was the father of Darius? Of Parysatis? What is the syllable γι in

πρεσβύτερος μὲν Ἀρταξέρξης, νεώτερος δὲ Κῦρος.

γίγνονται (123)? The reduplication prefixed to the Pres. is retained only in what two tenses? What effect has this syllable on the simple root or stem of the verb?[10] What is the root (123)? When does the excluded ε reappear?[11] How from the stem γεν is the Fut. γενήσομαι formed? The Fut. being formed from the stem by appending the tense characteristic σ and the ending, the regular Fut. of the stem γεν would be γέν-σ-ομαι, — what objection to such a form? Was the combination of σ and a liquid euphonious to a Grecian ear? What then is done in forming the Fut. of this word, to obviate the harshness of the sound?[12] How is the Pres. γίγνονται used here (152, 4)? What advantage has such a present tense over a past? Stem of παῖδες? Nom.? What becomes of the δ in the Nom.? Accent of the Gen. and Dat. Sing.? Principle (33, III., b)? Peculiarity of accent in Gen. Pl. (33, III., *Exceptions*)? Dat. Pl.? What letter is there dropped, and why? Any other form besides δύο? Can δύο and δύω be used indiscriminately? Difference of usage?[13] What English word from δύο? Had Darius but two children? How many? Why then does Xenophon mention but two here? Had he any occasion to speak of more than two? The comparative πρεσβύτερος, how formed (50, III.)? Pure stem of the positive? Why the comparative used? How many objects are brought into view always by the comparative? What is the office of μέν here? Is it generally to be translated into English? With what particle does it correspond? How is the δέ following μέν to be generally translated? In

Ἐπεὶ δὲ ἠσθένει Δαρεῖος καὶ ὑπώπτευε τελευτὴν τοῦ

what kind of clauses or members, then, do μέν ... δέ stand?[14] What is their position in their respective members? Do they ever stand first? Declension of Ἀρταξέρξης? Vocative Sing.? Why (27)? Why νεώτερος and not νεότερος (50, I. a)? How are all superlatives accented in the Nom.? Why the accent on καὶ, μὲν, δὲ depressed (12, 1)? Of what word do Ἀρταξέρξης and Κῦρος denote the parts? Accent of Κῦρος in the Gen.? Ground for the change (11, 1, a, β)? Does the circumflex on the υ of Κῦρος denote that the vowel is long, or short, or neither (10, 3)? What does ἐπεί connect? What δέ? Composition of ἠσθένει? Why Impf.? By the Impf. does the writer state the *permanent condition* of the king, or the mere *fact* that he was sick? What past tense would state the *fact* simply? Are ὑπώπτευε and ἐβούλετο in the Impf. for the same reason as ἠσθένει, *viz.*, to denote the *permanency* of the state of mind which they respectively denote? Why has Δαρεῖος the circumflex on the penult, but Δαρείου above the acute? Composition of ὑπώπτευε? What has become of the final vowel of the preposition? Why? How is the ω to be explained? What has lengthened it from ο (86)? Force of the ὑπό in composition, — does it strengthen or diminish the meaning of the simple verb ὀπτεύω? What preposition in Latin has the same force as ὑπό here? Does the Latin word *suspicio* (sub + spicio) have the same meaning as ὑπώπτευε? What English word of the same signification, coming from the Latin? Is a *suspicion* a full view of a thing, or a partial one? Force of the article with βίου (148, 3)?

βίου, ἐβούλετο τὼ παῖδε ἀμφοτέρω παρεῖναι. Ὁ μὲν οὖν πρεσβύτερος παρὼν ἐτύγχανε· Κῦρον δὲ μετα-

If the word were *βιοῦ* instead of *βίου*, what would be the meaning? Do we give to words of the same form a different meaning by a change of accent? What does *rec′ord* mean? What *record′*? What part of ἐβούλετο is root? What is the first ε? Second? The syllable το? What is the Fut.? What letter must be appended to the stem to form the Fut. and Perf. (125, 4)? Why?[12] Why the article τώ (148, 3)? What number is παῖδε? Is the Dual always used when two objects are spoken of (147, R. 3)? The *form* παῖδε may be Nom., Acc., or Voc., — which is it here, and what determines it? Construction? What classes of verbs take an Inf. as their complement (171, 2, and for the Acc. παῖδε, 172)? Derivation of ἀμφοτέρω? Composition of παρεῖναι? What has become of the final vowel of the preposition? Root of εἶναι in παρεῖναι? Whence comes the ει?[15] From what old Inf. ending does the ναι of παρεῖναι come (206, 11)? Rule for accentuation of infinitives in ναι (84, 4, a)? Upon what does the Inf. παρεῖναι depend (171, 2, a)? What is its subject Acc.? In the sentence introduced by ἐπεί, there is a principal and a subordinate clause, — which is principal, and which subordinate (179, 2)? Is the clause commencing with ἐπεί and ending with *βίου*, a substantive, adjective, or adverbial clause (179, 3)?[16] Does *οὖν* ever stand at the beginning of its clause? To what does it here refer; *i. e.*, of what does it denote an inference or consequence? Is it stronger or weaker than ἄρα?[17] From what does παρών come?

πέμπεται ἀπὸ τῆς ἀρχῆς ἧς αὐτὸν σατράπην ἐποίησε,

What is its relation to ἐτύγχανε (175, 3)? Does ἐτύγχανε here mean "happened," or does it signify "coincidence," having an adverbial force, and with παρών to be translated *was at that time, just then, present?* Root of ἐτύγχανε? Whence comes the γ (121, b)? The syllable αν (121, a)? From what stem is the Fut. τεύξομαι formed (121, 16)? From what the Perf. τετύχηκα? Why must an ε be appended to the stem τυχ to form the Perf.? Could a euphonic Perf. be formed without assuming the ε? Is δέ after Κῦρον adversative or continuative; *i. e.*, does it mean *but* or *and?* Force of μετα in μεταπέμπεται? Does the English use *after* in that sense? Why the verb in the middle voice? Difference between the Act. and Mid. of this verb? Fut. Mid.? What elements form the ψ? What kind of a Pres. is it? Why is the Pres. used rather than a past tense? What is the general rule for the accentuation of the verb? Does the accent of μεταπέμπεται correspond with that rule? How are the regular prepositions accented, on the penult or the ultimate? Why the article with ἀρχῆς? Why τῆς and ἀρχῆς circumflexed on the ultimate? What cases of oxytones in the Nom. are uniformly perispomenon (26, 5, a)? From what does τῆς come? What must be the assumed or ideal form from which it comes?[18] What did the ἀρχή of Cyrus embrace? Construction of ἧς? Of αὐτόν and σατράπην (160, 3)? Can σατράπην properly be considered in apposition with αὐτόν? Which of these two accusatives stands in the relation of a predicate? Peculiarity in the inflection of

καὶ στρατηγὸν δὲ αὐτὸν ἀπέδειξε πάντων ὅσοι εἰς Κασ-

αὐτόν (60)? Is σατράπην a word of Greek origin? From what language is it derived? Verb stem of ἐποίησε? Tense stem? Tense characteristic (79, 1)? What actual relation of time does ἐποίησε express? What tense would the English naturally use here? Why does not the Greek? Did the Greek prefer the Aor. to the less pliant Plupf. except where great precision of time was required?[19] Force of καί before στρατηγόν? Upon what word does its force fall? With what word does it contrast στρατηγόν? When the combination καὶ δέ occurs in a sentence, what is the position of the word to which καί refers, or on which its force falls?[20] Composition of στρατηγόν? What letter would regularly stand instead of η? How is the change to be explained?[21] Government of στρατηγόν and αὐτόν? Pres. of ἀπέδειξε? Composition? Force of ἀπό? Root of the simple word? What is added to the root to form the Pres.? When is νυ and when νυυ added to the root (128, II.)? In what tenses is νυ or νυυ retained? What are the elements in the ξ of ἀπέδειξε? Whence comes the σ in the ξ? What is the tense characteristic of the Fut., first Aor. Act., etc, (79, 1)? Stem of πάντων? What letter rejects ντ in the Nom. Sing. masculine? What is that σ?[22] How does the accent of πάντων differ from that of monosyllabic words of the third Dec. (33, III. *Exceptions*)? Is it then an exception to an exception? To what rule is it an exception? Does πᾶς follow the accentuation of monosyllabic words, except in this case? Why does πάντων stand after ἀπέδειξε, and not with στρατηγόν, by

τωλοῦ πεδίον ἀθροίζονται. Ἀναβαίνει οὖν ὁ Κῦρος λαβὼν Τισσαφέρνην ὡς φίλον· καὶ τῶν Ἑλλήνων δὲ

which it is governed? What is the general position of the antecedent with respect to the relative, near or remote? Would the relative οἵ have the same force as ὅσοι here? What is the difference? Which contains the idea of number? Εἰς appears without an accent; is it a proclitic or enclitic? What is meant by a proclitic (13)? From the circumflex on the Gen. ending of Καστωλοῦ, what must be the accent of the Nom.? Where was Castolus? Πεδίον is allied to what word, meaning *foot?* The neuter noun πεδίον is paroxytone; is any neuter noun ever oxytone? Derivation of ἀθροίζονται? Why the Pres.? Does it refer to their assembling once, or from year to year? Why ἀναβαίνει and not the simple βαίνει? What feature in the position of the place to which he was going, requires the compound form? To what place was he going? Root of βαίνω? What letters are inserted to form the Pres.? Into what letter is the stem vowel changed in the Fut.? Why the Pres. used here instead of the Aor.? To what does οὖν refer, to the same fact as the previous οὖν? Stem of λαβών? How from the stem λαβ is the Pres. λαμβάνω formed (121, a and b)? How is the μ before β to be explained (8, 6)? Is the Fut. in the Act. or Mid. form? What change takes place in the stem vowel in the Fut.? Rule for accent of λαβών (84, 3, a)? Could the Latin express λαβὼν Τισσαφέρνην in the same way? Why not? Has the Latin any past Act. participle? How may it be translated into Latin? Of what two declensions is Τισσα-

ἔχων ὁπλίτας ἀνέβη τριακοσίους, ἄρχοντα δὲ αὐτῶν Ξενίαν Παῤῥάσιον.

φέρνης? Of which is the Nom.? Who was Tissaphernes? What post had he held previous to Cyrus's arrival in Asia Minor? Construction of φίλον? Is there reason to suppose that Cyrus regarded Tissaphernes as a friend, or did he take him because he feared he might intrigue against him in his absence? Force of καί before τῶν? Is it a connective here? What is the connective in this clause? What word does Ἑλλήνων restrict or explain? What other word explains ὁπλίτας? The use of ἔχων here, and frequently elsewhere, corresponds nearly with what English preposition? Fut. of ἔχω? Why the Fut. ἕξω (aspirated) when the Pres. is ἔχω (8, 10)? Aor. Act. of ἔχω? Impf.? What peculiarity in that tense? How many verbs have the same (87, 3)? Voc. Sing. of ὁπλίτας? Accent? Why properispomenon in Voc., but not here? Is the ending ας long or short? Accent of Gen. Pl. (26, 4, γ)? Principle? What nouns have α and what η in the Voc. Sing. (27)? From what noun is ὁπλίτας derived? What is the ε in ἀνέβη? What has it excluded? Is ἀνέβη transitive or intransitive? Is this tense formed regularly? Like what class of verbs? Stem of ἄρχοντα? What letter of the stem is dropped in the Nom. (35)? Dat. Pl. of the word? What two letters are dropped? What letter rejects these? What change takes place as a compensation for the letters dropped (8, 8)? Would τούτων be more or less emphatic than αὐτῶν here?[23] If there were no pronouns, what word must be used here instead

Ἐπεὶ δὲ ἐτελεύτησε Δαρεῖος καὶ κατέστη εἰς τὴν βασιλείαν Ἀρταξέρξης, Τισσαφέρνης διαβάλλει τὸν

of αὐτῶν? Dec. of Ξενίαν? Where was Parrhasia, from which Zenias came?

What does ἐπειδή connect? What δέ? Derivation of ἐτελεύτησε? Τελευτή from what? To what tense is the Aor. after adverbs of time, like ἐπειδή, equivalent? Why is not the Plupf. used, then (152, R. 6)? Which of the tenses is the less stiff and flexible? What is the principal clause of which ἐπειδὴ δὲ ἐτελεύτησε is the subordinate? In what year did Darius die? Composition of κατέστη? Stem of the simple verb (128, I. a)? Whence comes the aspirate ἱ of the Pres.?[24] What is this ἱ? In what tenses retained? Pres. of κατέστη? Why the τ of κατα changed into ϑ (8, 2)? How is τ brought into juxtaposition with the aspirated ἱ (90, 1)? Difference between the first and second Aor. of ἵστημι (150, 2)? Why the article with βασιλείαν? From the accent on βασιλείαν what may be inferred in regard to the quantity of the ultimate (10, 5)? If the ultimate were short, what would the accent be? How is βασιλεια, *kingdom*, distinguished from βασιλεια, *queen*? Root of διαβάλλω? Is it a mute or liquid verb (111)? Whence the second λ (111, 2)? What becomes of it in the Fut.? Are any strengthening letters retained beyond the Pres. and Impf.? How comes the Future of this and other liquid verbs to be circumflexed? What would be the full form of the Fut. of this word prior to any syncopation and contraction (111 R. 1)? What letter is syncopated? After the syncopation what takes place?

Κῦρον πρὸς τὸν ἀδελφὸν ὡς ἐπιβουλεύοι αὐτῷ. Ὁ δὲ

Why do not liquid verbs form the future in -σω, like other verbs? Is the combination of a liquid and σ, as βάλσω, euphonious? Does βάλλω form a first or second Aor. Act.? What is its Aor. Act.? How formed? Do verbs generally have more than one Aor. Act.? Is there usually any difference of *meaning* between a first and second Aor. (for exceptions see 150, 2)? When a verb is said to be in the first or second Aor., is anything more meant than that each has a form peculiar to itself? Peculiarity in the Perf. of βάλλω (117, 2)? Reason for this metathesis? Could a euphonic Perf. be formed from the unchanged stem βαλ? Primary meaning of διαβάλλει? Force of δια? What kind of a Pres.? What different cases does πρός govern? Why the article with ἀδελφόν (148, 3)? In what case is the accent of ἀδελφός anomalous (28, R. 2)? What does ὡς connect? With reference to accentuation, what is it called (13, c)? Why ἐπιβουλεύοι in the Opt.? When the verb of the principal clause is in the present tense, is the verb of the dependent clause usually in the Opt. (181, R.)? Why is it so here? Διαβάλλει, though in the Present, is equivalent to what tense? May ἐπιβουλεύοι also be considered in *oratio obliqua*, there being a verb of *saying* understood: "saying that he was plotting against him"? Why are διαβάλλει and ἐπιβουλεύοι paroxytones, while ἀπέδειξε and ἐτελεύτησε are proparoxytones? Construction of αὐτῷ? May it be considered the limiting Dative? What word does it limit, and what is meant when it is said to limit that word? If αὐτῷ were removed,

πείθεταί τε καὶ συλλαμβάνει Κῦρον ὡς ἀποκτενῶν·

would the expression be definite? Might αὐτῷ be also considered the Dat. of disadvantage? What is the difference between the limiting Dat. and the Dat. of advantage or disadvantage (161, 2, c, δ)? What part of speech is ὁ? How used here? Was its earliest use that of an article or a pronoun? Is its pronominal use frequent in Attic Greek?[25] Fut. of πείθεται? What becomes of the θ? What letter rejects it? What is that σ (79, 1)? Second Perf. Act.? What class of verbs have οι in the second Perf. (102, 4)? Have τε καί the same force that καί alone would have; *i. e.*, is the idea of the verbs brought out more or less prominently by τε καί than it would have been by καί (178. 3)? How can the force of the two be expressed in English? Composition of συλλαμβάνει? How does the ν of the preposition become λ (8, 4)? But what will this λ become in the Impf.? Does the cause which changed it into λ exist in the Impf.? What influence has the preposition upon the meaning of the simple word? Does it imply the combined action of several persons, or the concentrated effort of one? Perf. Act. of the verb? What peculiarity in the form of the Perf.? How many verbs have this peculiarity (88, 4)? What would be the regular reduplication, instead of εἰ? Whence comes the syllable εἰ?[26] Force of ὡς before ἀποκτενῶν? Does it denote *purpose*? Does not the Fut. Part. denote *purpose* without ὡς? If ὡς were omitted here, would the action indicated by ἀποκτενῶν be presented as a *fact*, or as a *representation*,— something which Artaxerxes is represented or considered

ἡ δὲ μήτηρ ἐξαιτησαμένη αὐτὸν ἀποπέμπει πάλιν ἐπὶ τὴν ἀρχήν. Ὁ δ' ὡς ἀπῆλθε κινδυνεύσας καὶ ἀτιμασ-

as intending to do? With ὡς, which of these meanings is given; *i.e.*, does ὡς ἀποκτενῶν denote the writer's view, so that he is responsible for it as a historical statement, or is it the view, thought, intention, of Artaxerxes?[27] From what Pres. does ἀποκτενῶν come? What becomes of the ι in the Fut.? How does that ι come to stand in the Pres. (111, 2)? What is the Perf. generally used in Attic? Why that form (111, 5)? Why the article with μήτηρ? In what cases does it reject ε? In what one assume α? Which have an irregular accent (39)? Why ἐξαιτησαμένη in the Mid. voice? Force of the preposition? Why ἐξ and not ἐκ? Has the Act. ἀποπέμπει just the same relation as the Mid. would? Which denotes the idea of *sending away* merely, and which that of *sending away from one's self*? Though the two voices are thus different, might either be used here? Primary meaning of πάλιν? What different cases does ἐπί govern? How is ἀρχή accented in the Gen. and Dat.? On what principle? How are all genitives Pl. of the first Dec. accented? Why? Are the endings of all nouns of the first Dec. the same in the Dual and Plural? Is it so in the Sing.? Is δ' before ὡς adversative or continuative? What is the mark after the δ'? What does it indicate? Does ὡς here have the same meaning as ὡς before φίλον above? What is its meaning? What does it connect? From what Pres. does ἀπῆλθε come? From what root? What connection has it with ἔρχομαι? Any in form? The Fut. of ἔρχομαι for Attic Greek? Why

θείς, βουλεύεται ὅπως μήποτε ἔτι ἔσται ἐπὶ τῷ ἀδελ-

the different tenses from different roots?[28] Full form, instead of ἀπῆλθε? Why not accented on the antepenult (84, 2)? Why properispomenon (10, 5, b)? From what noun is κινδυνεύσας derived? Rule for accentuation (84, R. 3)? From the acute on the penult what may be inferred in regard to the quantity of the ultimate? What makes the final syllable long in all such participles (190, e)? What two letters have been dropped? What relation does this participle denote, that of time, cause, conditionality, or what (176)? What is the Latin conjunction corresponding to καί? Composition of ἀτιμασθείς? From what does τιμάω come? From what τιμή? Primary meaning of τίω? In how many senses is α prefixed to words? What would be the full ending instead of -είς in ἀτιμασθείς? What two letters are dropped in the ending, — the same as in κινδυνεύσας? Why then the ending -ας in one word and -είς in the other?[29] What is the θ in ἀτιμασθείς? Rule for accentuation (84, 3, c)? What Latin participle is equivalent to the Greek Aorist? To what two tenses in Greek does the Latin Perf. correspond? Meaning of the word *Aorist*? Composition? Why βουλεύεται in the Mid.? Difference between Act. and Mid. of this word? Which means *to give advice*, and which *to get advice* or *deliberate*? How is ὅπως related to πῶς; in what kind of clauses is each used (63, b)? Origin of the ὁ in ὅπως?[30] Is ὅπως followed by any other mood than the Indic. Fut., as here? What? With what class of verbs is the Fut. the usual tense (181, 4)? What does ὅπως connect? Why μήποτε

φῷ, ἀλλ', ἢν δύνηται, βασιλεύσει ἀντ' ἐκείνου. Πα-

and not οὔποτε (177, 5)? What force does πότε give to μή? Root from which ἔσται comes? Full form (137, R. 1)? Why the accent of ἐπί depressed? Why the article with ἀδελφῷ? Why perispomenon? What is the history of the ι *subscript*?[31] From what does ἀλλ' come? In its origin is it an adjective or a conjunction? What does the mark after it denote? Peculiarity in its accentuation here? To what other words does the same principle apply (12, 3)? If it followed the accentuation of oxytones whose ultimate is elided, what would be the accentuation of ἀλλ' here? How does ἀλλα the conjunction differ from ἀλλα, *other things*? Are they both from the same word? How does the position of ἀλλά (*but*) in a sentence differ from δέ? What two other forms equivalent to ἤν? In what part of their clause do ἐάν, ἤν, and ἄν (*if*) stand? By what mood are they followed? How does ἤν here differ from the first Pers. Sing. Indic. Impf. of εἶμι (137)? What is implied by ἤν with the subjunctive [185, 2 (3)]? How differing from εἰ with the Indic. or Opt. [185, 2 (1) and (4)]? What is the η in δύνηται (79, R.)? What would be the corresponding vowel of the Indic.? What is the syllable -ται, and what is its office? In what part of the word, then, is the *meaning* found? Derivation of βασιλεύσει? The penult is long, why not circumflexed? What one condition is wanting in order to its being circumflexed? What is the σ before ει? Are verbs in -εύω generally transitive or intransitive? How is the absence of the accent on ἀντ' to be explained (12, 3)? This is like what

ρύσατις μὲν δὴ ἡ μήτηρ ὑπῆρχε τῷ Κυρῷ, φιλοῦσα αὐτὸν μᾶλλον ἢ τὸν βασιλεύοντα Ἀρταξέρξην. Ὅστις

other word above? Peculiarity in the declension of ἐκείνου (60)? What previous word has the same peculiarity? With what Latin pronoun does ἐκείνου correspond? Stem of Παρύσατις? What rejects the δ? What is the final σ? With what particle does μέν correspond? Force of δή? Would *evidently*, or *as is evident*, express the meaning? Composition of ὑπῆρχε? Why the final vowel of the preposition rejected? How does the α of ἄρχω become η (86)? Which augment is η? Why called the *temporal* augment? Why is the accent on the penult and not on the antepenult (84, 2)? If the accent is on the penult, and the penult long and the ultimate short, what must the accent be (10, 5, b)? Why ὑπῆρχε in the Impf.? Does it denote a single effort in his behalf, or continued efforts? By what principle is Κυρῷ in the Dat.? From what noun is φιλοῦσα derived? How is the syllable ου to be explained? What would be the regular form previous to any changes? What vowel is dropped? What two consonants? Why? What change then takes place in the ο? Why (8, 8)? What would be the regular form of the comparative instead of μᾶλλον? By what principle is the ι of μάλιον changed into λ? Does not the second λ of ἄλλος come in the same way? Does assimilation take place in the Latin word corresponding with ἄλλος? What word would the Latin use for ἤ after μᾶλλον? How does ὅστις differ from the simple ὅς? Which is the more general or comprehensive word? What Latin word would express the force of ὅστις? How many

δ' ἀφικνοῖτο τῶν παρὰ βασιλέως πρὸς αὐτόν, πάντας οὕτω διατιθεὶς ἀπεπέμπετο ὥσθ' ἑαυτῷ μᾶλλον φίλους

different declensions in ὅστις (62)? How many in ὅς alone? Does ὅστις denote a single individual, or has it a collective sense? Composition of ἀφικνοῖτο? Why is π of the preposition changed into φ? Stem of the simple word? How from the stem ἱκ is ἱκνέομαι obtained (120, 2)? In what tenses is the syllable νε retained? From what is the Fut. ἵξομαι formed? What are the elements in the ξ in the Fut. (8, 7)? Force of ἀπο in ἀφικνοῖτο? How else is the same relation expressed here? What does the Opt. mode denote? Some texts have the Impf. Indic., — what would that denote? Where the introductory clause, with the Opt. mode, denotes indefinite frequency or a repeated action (*as often as, whenever, whoever from time to time*), what is the tense of the verb in the principal clause (182, 8, c)? Why is this so?[32] What verb in this sentence illustrates that principle? Construction of τῶν? How would τῶν παρὰ βασιλέως be literally translated?[33] Primary meaning of παρά? What does it show the relation between? What is the double relation of παρὰ βασιλέως here?[34] Why βασιλέως without the article? What does πρός show the relation between? To what does πάντας refer? How can the plural πάντας refer to the singular ὅστις? By what two words is πάντας governed? Derivation of οὕτω? When οὕτω and when οὕτως used (7, 2)? Composition of διατιθείς? Force of δια? What is the syllable τι (127, 2)? Why is it not θι (8, 9)? Stem of τίθημι (128, I.)? Rule for accent of διατιθείς (84, 3, c)? How is the syllable -είς

εἶναι ἢ βασιλεῖ. Καὶ τῶν παρ' ἑαυτῷ δὲ βαρβάρων ἐπεμελεῖτο ὡς πολεμεῖν τε ἱκανοὶ εἴησαν καὶ εὐνοϊκῶς

obtained (131, g, and 8, 8)? How does the Middle ἀπε-πέμπετο differ from the Act. ἀποπέμπει above? Which implies the idea of sending away without any reference to the person from whom one is sent? Can our language distinguish between these two voices in translating, except by a periphrasis? How is the form ὥσθ' to be explained? Composition? Has the τε any force? How came it to be associated with ὡς?[35] What different modes follow ὥστε (186)? Difference between it when followed by the Inf., Indic., and Opt.? Construction of ἑαυτῷ? What other form (57)? Composition? Construction of φίλους? Is it the subject Acc. of εἶναι or the predicate? What is the subject Acc.? On what does εἶναι depend (186, 1, a) From what is βασιλεῖ contracted (41)? Force of καί before τῶν? *Moreover*, in addition to what? What word connects this sentence with the preceding? Why does the article τῶν which belongs to βαρβάρων, stand before παρ' ἑαυτῷ? This position makes παρ' ἑαυτῷ sustain what relation to βαρβάρων? Whom did the Greeks call barbarians? How can the τῶν παρ' ἑαυτῷ βαρβάρων be translated literally into English, so as to indicate the attributive or adjective force of παρ' ἑαυτῷ?[36] How is the absence of the accent of παρ' to be explained? Government of βαρβάρων? Rule (158, 6, I. b)? What is the double relation of βαρβάρων here? Besides its connection with ἐπεμελεῖτο, of what verb is it the subject? Could it have been omitted entirely as a Gen., and have been only

ἔχοιεν αὐτῷ. Τὴν δὲ Ἑλληνικὴν δύναμιν ἤθροιζεν ὡς

in the Nom.; *i. e.*, is it not made by attraction the object of the verb of the principal clause, instead of the subject of the verb of the subordinate clause? How would the sentence be then translated? Why ἐπεμελεῖτο Impf.? How is the circumflex on the penult to be explained? What would be the accent before contraction? Are all contracted syllables circumflexed? What does ὡς connect? Difference between ὡς with and without the accent? From what noun does πολεμεῖν come? On what depend? Why perispomenon [11, 2, (2), (b), (β)]? Force of τε after it? With what particle is τε correlative? How may the force of τε .... καί be expressed in English (178, 3)? What would be lost to the sentence if τε were omitted? On what general principle is εἴησαν here in the Opt. (181, 2)? When the verb of the principal clause is a historical tense, what is generally the mode of the verb of the subordinate clause? What other form could be used besides εἴησαν (137)? Composition of εὐνοϊκῶς? Ἔχειν with an adverb is equivalent to what other verb?[37] How would εὐνοϊκῶς ἔχοιεν be translated literally? Fut. of ἔχω? Why has the ἐ an aspirate in the Fut. and not in the Pres. (8, 10)? Construction of αὐτῷ? What expression does it limit or restrict? Why does the article τήν stand with Ἑλληνικήν and not with δύναμιν? Does the force of the article as here placed fall on Ἑλληνικήν or δύναμιν (148, 9, a)? With what does its present position contrast Ἑλληνικήν? How is the Gen. Sing. of δύναμιν accented? Principle (46)? Why ἤθροιζεν in the Impf.? Does the writer mean to

μάλιστα ἐδύνατο ἐπικρυπτόμενος, ὅπως ὅτι ἀπαρασκευ-ότατον λάβοι βασιλέα. Ὧδε οὖν ἐποιεῖτο τὴν συλλο-

state a historical fact, or the course of procedure from day to day? If merely the historical fact was to be stated, what tense would have been used? Force of ὡς before μάλιστα? Upon what word does its force fall?[38] Is some part of δύναμαι always expressed, as here, when ὡς is joined with the superlative?[39] What is the second Pers. Sing. of ἐδύνατο? How is the form obtained? What letter is syncopated, and what contraction takes place (comp. ἵστασο and ἵστω, 133)? Why ἐπικρυπτόμενος in the Mid. voice? How differing from the Act.? What was he concealing,— himself, his own measures, or those of others? Pure characteristic of ἐπικρύπτω? Impure (104, 1)? What does ὅπως connect? Why is it here followed by the Opt., but above by the Fut. Indic.? Composition of ὅτι? Its force or office here? How can clauses like this be analyzed to show in what way ὅτι has a strengthening force?[40] Composition of ἀπαρασκευότατον? Why is the vowel of the antepenult ο, and not ω? When is ο, and when ω, used in the comparative and superlative (50, I. a)? Why λάβοι in the Opt. (181, 2)? Difference between ὧδε and οὕτως? Which refers to what precedes, and which to what follows? Why ἐποιεῖτο in the Impf.? Was the act described done at once, or was it a continuous process? Could the writer, however, *narratively* have used the Aor. here (152, 10)? Why the verb in the Mid. voice? What would ἐποίει συλλογήν mean?[41] Composition of συλ-λογήν? Why the article with it? Why two λ's? Why

γήν. Ὁπόσας εἶχε φυλακὰς ἐν ταῖς πόλεσι, παρήγγειλε τοῖς φρουράρχοις ἑκάστοις λαμβάνειν ἄνδρας Πελοπον-

ὁπόσας, and not πόσας? What is the appropriate use of each (63, a)? Peculiarity of εἶχε in its augment? How many verbs have the same (87, 3)? Does φυλακάς here come from φυλακη or φυλαξ? How determined? Difference between φυλακάς and φύλακας? Why ἐν without an accent? Why the article with πόλεσι? Are cities in general referred to, or such as were under his control, and hence particular ones? What has become of the stem vowel ι of πόλεσι? In what cases only is it retained? What vowel takes its place in the other cases (46)? Composition of παρήγγειλε? What rejects the final vowel of the preposition? Whence comes the η? What is the Fut. of ἀγγέλλω? In what two respects does it differ from the Pres? How is the circumflex of the ultimate to be explained? Why is one of the λ's dropped in the Fut.? Why does not this verb form its Fut. in σω? Why is σ rejected in liquid verbs? How is the ει in the penult of παρήγγειλε to be explained (111, 3)? Composition of φρουράρχοις? Why Dat. [161, 2, a, (ε)]? Would the clause ὁπόσας εἶχε, etc., or παρήγγειλε, etc., regularly stand first? Which is the relative clause, and which the antecedent? If the antecedent clause were placed first, in which clause and in what case would φυλακάς regularly stand? In what other way, then, could the sentence ὁπόσας .... φρουράρχοις be expressed?[42] Upon what does λαμβάνειν depend? What classes of verbs take an Inf. for their complement or object (171, 2)? What becomes of the η of ἀνήρ in all cases

νησίους ὅτι πλείστους καὶ βελτίστους, ὡς ἐπιβουλεύοντος Τισσαφέρνους ταῖς πόλεσι. Καὶ γὰρ ἦσαν αἱ

except the Voc. Sing. (36)? Is the accentuation of the word regular? Origin of the δ in ἄνδρας? Is it usual in Greek for more than two consonants to come together? Why then an additional consonant inserted here? Between what letters may a medial mute be inserted to soften the pronunciation?[43] Any instance of a letter similarly inserted in Latin?[44] Any in English?[45] Composition of Πελοποννησίους? What, then, is the meaning of the word? Why was the order given to take Peloponnesians? Was it merely because they were distinguished for their bravery? Had Cyrus favored the Peloponnesians or the Athenians during the Peloponnesian war? From what party, therefore, would he be most likely to obtain forces? Force of ὅτι before πλείστους? Office of ὡς with ἐπιβουλεύοντος,—does it imply that the action denoted by the participle was actually taking place, or that Cyrus merely *pretended* that it was taking place? Does ὡς indicate, then, that the participle expresses Cyrus's view, or that of the historian? How may ὡς be rendered in such cases?[46] What would ἐπιβουλεύοντος without ὡς mean here?[47] Dec. of Τισσαφέρνους? Construction? What is meant by the term *absolute*, when a word is said to be in the Gen. absolute? Why ν appended to πόλεσι (7, 1, a)? Force of καί before γάρ? Does it connect what immediately precedes with what follows, or something understood with what follows? Would the English generally translate it in such cases?[48] What is the purport of the clause to be supplied? Com-

Ἰωνικαὶ πόλεις Τισσαφέρνους τὸ ἀρχαῖον ἐκ βασιλέως δεδομέναι, τότε δ' ἀφεστήκεσαν πρὸς Κῦρον πᾶσαι πλὴν

position of γάρ? Peculiarity in the inflection of the second Pers. Sing. of ἦσαν (137)? What other words retain a similar feature of the Epic dialect (comp. φήμι, οἶδα, 135 and 143)? Why ἦσαν in the Impf. here? Any difference between αἱ Ἰωνικαὶ πόλεις and Ἰωνικαὶ αἱ πόλεις? What (148, 9, a and b)? As it stands in the text, does the article give emphasis to the Ἰωνικαί or πόλεις? Construction of Τισσαφέρνους (158, 2)? Is the article often joined with a neuter adjective, as τό with ἀρχαῖον here, where an adverbial relation is expressed? Is ἐκ the preposition commonly used with Pass. verbs to denote the agent? What one is generally used? But does ἐκ express a different relation from what ὑπό would here? Which denotes the more intimate connection of the agent with the act of giving? Can the English, however, express the distinction? In δεδομέναι, what is the simple stem? What is the first δ? The ε after it? What is -μέναι? Rule for the accentuation of the participle (84, 4, c)? Is the stem vowel of the Perf. Act. and Pass. of δίδωμι the same? What is that of each? Is τότε a demonstrative or relative adverb? What is the corresponding relative adverb (63, b)? How does τότε differ from τοτέ? What time is here referred to by τότε? Is δέ continuative or adversative? How determined? Composition of ἀφεστήκεσαν? Why the π changed into φ? Force of ἀπο? What is the simple word from which the verb is formed? Stem of ἵστημι (128, I, a)? Whence comes the aspirated ἱ before σ? By what principle is the ε

Μιλήτου. Ἐν Μιλήτῳ δὲ Τισσαφέρνης προαισθόμενος τὰ αὐτὰ ταῦτα βουλευομένους, ἀποστῆναι πρὸς Κῦρον,

of the Perf. (ἕστηκα) aspirated?[49] Tense of ἀφεστήκεσαν? But is the Plupf. relation the prominent one? Does the writer wish to fix attention upon the fact that they had revolted, or that they are now in a *state* of revolt? How can the Plupf. do this?[50] What other ending of the third Pers. Pl. Plupf. besides -εσαν (82, 1)? Why is πᾶσαι placed the last in its clause? Is it desirable that it should stand as near as possible to the word which corrects or restricts it? What is that corrective word? How can the sentence be translated so as to preserve the position of πᾶσαι? Is πλήν strictly a preposition? Government of Μιλήτου (157)? Where was Miletus? Tense of προαισθόμενος? From what Pres.? What has become of the syllable αν in προαισθάνομαι? Stem of the verb? How is the Fut. formed (121, a)? Force of the preposition προ? Foreseeing, — seeing before what? Is the final vowel retained by rule or exception? What is the rule and what the exception (90, 1)? Meaning of αὐτά preceded by the article (60, R.)? Τὰ αὐτὰ ταῦτα, *these same things*, — the same as what? Composition of ταῦτα? When has οὗτος in its different cases ου in the penult, and when αυ?[51] If the article τά were omitted before αὐτά here, what would αὐτὰ ταῦτα mean? What Latin pronoun corresponds with αὐτά? What with ταῦτα? Why βουλευομένους in the Mid. voice? With what agreeing? Is it necessary to supply a word, as τινάς, or may the participle be said to contain an indefinite pronoun in itself? Would it be according to the

τοὺς μὲν αὐτῶν ἀπέκτεινε, τοὺς δ' ἐξέβαλεν. Ὁ δέ Κῦρος ὑπολαβὼν τοὺς φεύγοντας, συλλέξας στράτευμα ἐπολι-

usage of the language to substitute an Inf. for the Part. βουλευομένους? Why not? Why is a Part. required here (175, 1, a)? What relation does βουλευομένους sustain to προαισθόμενος?[52] Of what are the words ἀποστῆναι πρὸς Κῦρον expletive? What particle does the English use in translating them, which neither the Greek nor Latin employs?[53] What is the syllable -ναι in ἀποστῆναι? In forming the Pres. Inf. Act. of verbs in μι, is ναι appended to the short or long characteristic vowel? To which in the second Aor. (130, f)? Office of μέν after τούς? Has the English an equivalent particle? How can its force be indicated in English? Where is the correlative of μέν? Is τούς here merely an article, or has it its original pronominal force?[54] Construction of αὐτῶν? In the oblique cases, when αὐτός stands alone, not agreeing with any word, is it emphatic, or has it merely the force of a personal pronoun (169, 7)? Tense of ἀπέκτεινε, — Aor. or Impf.? How determined? Is the form of both in all respects the same, and the accent the same? From the nature of the case, what tense would it seem to be? Compared with ἐξέβαλεν, what additional means is there for the decision? Is the regular Perf. Act. of this word used by Attic writers? Why not (111, 5)? What form is used? Composition of ἐξέβαλεν? Why ἐξ, and not ἐκ? Origin of the second λ in the Pres. (111, 2)? Peculiarity in Perf. Act. (117, 2)? Why the article with φεύγοντας (148, 6)? Two forms of the Fut. of φεύγω? Is

όρκει Μίλητον καὶ κατὰ γῆν καὶ κατὰ θάλατταν, καὶ ἐπειρᾶτο κατάγειν τοὺς ἐκπεπτωκότας. Καὶ αὕτη αὖ

its Perf. Act. the regular Perf. (116, 3)? Composition of συλλέξας? The first λ, how explained (8, 4)? What becomes of that λ in the Indic. Aor.? The elements in the ξ? Perf. Act. of λέγω in its signification here? In the sense of *to say* (88, 4, and R. 2)? What relation of time do ὑπολαβών and συλλέξας sustain to ἐπολιόρκει? Can they be rendered by finite verbs into English? By what tense then? Why are not finite verbs used instead of these participles (176, R. 1)? Do the participles express the principal action or the accompanying circumstances here? What word expresses the principal action? From what verb does στράτευμα come? Why without the article? Stem? On what principle is final τ rejected (32, 2)? Composition of ἐπολιόρκει? Why Impf.? Force of καί before the first κατά (178, 3, b)? Is it necessary to the general sense? What would be lost by the omission? How would the clause be translated without it, and how with it? Does κατά govern any other case than the Acc.? How does the Acc. after κατά here differ from the same words in the Gen.? Which case expresses the idea of *extension over, throughout,* and of course the stronger idea? Does the English say by *land and sea* as the Greek, or the reverse? The corresponding Latin for κατὰ γῆν καὶ κατὰ θάλατταν? Does the arrangement of the Latin words correspond with the Greek or English? Derivation of θάλατταν? Origin of the θ? Why ἐπειρᾶτο in the Impf.? Is the reason the same as for ἐπολιόρκει? Is not, likewise, the

ἄλλη πρόφασις ἦν αὐτῷ τοῦ ἀθροίζειν στράτευμα. Πρὸς δὲ βασιλέα πέμπων ἠξίου, ἀδελφὸς ὢν αὐτοῦ,

idea of *endeavoring* strengthened by the Impf., since what one is engaged upon is not accomplished, but he is *endeavoring* to do or accomplish (152, R. 4, d)? Is not the same strengthening force of the Impf. seen in the Impf. of *μένω*, *soleo*, etc.? Stem of *ἐκπεπτωκότας* (123)? What is the syllable *πι* of the Pres.? In the Pres. what becomes of *ε* of the stem? What rejects it? When does it reappear? Is the *ω* of the Perf. regular? Force of the Perf. Part. here? Does it denote a past action, or a present state or result (152, R. 2)? To what does *αὕτη* refer? If to the preceding statements, why is it not in the neuter gender according to the rule? But to what word is its gender conformed (147, R. 1)? What is such a conforming of the gender to that of the noun called?[55] If the word with which *αὕτη* agrees were omitted, what then would be its gender? Would that be according to the general rule? Is the position of *αὕτη* between *καί* and *αὖ* emphatic or unemphatic?[56] Origin of the second λ in *ἄλλη*? Does the same assimilation occur in the corresponding Latin word? Peculiarity in the inflection of *ἄλλος* (60)? Composition of *πρόφασις*? Construction of *αὐτῷ* (161, 2, a)? To what does the article *τοῦ* belong (173, 1)? The Inf. *ἀθροίζειν* by the article *τοῦ* becoming a noun, is governed by what word? Does it at the same time retain its properties as a verb (173, 1)? What property of the verb does it have here? Derivation of *ἠξίου*? Uncontracted form? Meaning here? Force of Impf.? What is its grammatical

δοϑῆναί οἱ ταύτας τὰς πόλεις μᾶλλον ἢ Τισσαφέρνην ἄρχειν αὐτῶν· καὶ ἡ μήτηρ συνέπραττεν αὐτῷ ταῦτα· ὥστε βασιλεὺς τῆς μὲν πρὸς ἑαυτὸν ἐπιβουλῆς οὐκ

object? Construction of ἀδελφός? Standing without the article, does it mean *a brother of his* (indefinite) or *his brother* (definite)? With the article what would it mean? What relation is expressed by the Part. ὤν, — time, cause, conditionality, or what (176, 1)? Of what does it express the cause or reason? What part of δοϑῆναι is stem (128, c)? What is ϑ (79, 1)? What is the remainder? Upon what does δοϑῆναι depend? Rule for accentuation (84, 4, a)? What cities are meant by ταύτας πόλεις? Construction of πόλεις (172)? How is the second λ in μᾶλλον to be explained? Does it originate like the second λ in ἄλλος? What would be the form before assimilation? On what does ἄρχειν depend? Government of αὐτῶν (158, 7, *a*)? Root of συνέπραττεν? How from the root πραγ is the Pres. πράττω formed? Whence comes the second τ (100, 1, a)? The first? What influence has the second τ upon the γ of the root?[57] Force of συν in συνέπραττεν? What is the form of the Pres.? Why is the ν of the preposition μ there (8, 6)? What is the final ν? Why is it used here (7, 1)? Why the verb in the Impf.? How is συνέπραττεν αὐτῷ ταῦτα literally translated? To what does ταῦτα refer? Why neuter gender? Why is ὥστε here followed by the Indic., and not by the Inf.? Is the consequence represented as something *actual*, a *fact*, or as something *supposed* or *possible* (186, 1, a)? Why does the article τῆς stand before πρὸς ἑαυτόν, and not with its

ᾐσθάνετο, Τισσαφέρνει δὲ ἐνόμιζε πολεμοῦντα αὐτὸν ἀμφὶ τὰ στρατεύματα δαπανᾶν· ὥστε οὐδὲν ἤχθετο

noun? What relation does this position of the article make πρὸς ἑαυτόν sustain to ἐπιβουλῆς (148, 8, last part)? How can the whole be translated so as to show this relation?[53] If, instead of the present position, it were written τῆς ἐπιβουλῆς τῆς πρὸς ἑαυτόν, would the meaning be the same or different (148, R. 8)? Government of ἐπιβουλῆς (158, 5, b)? Does αἰσθάνομαι usually govern the Acc. of the thing? Does the Gen. ἐπιβουλῆς express the same that the Acc. would? Does the Gen. mean that he did not perceive the plot as a whole, or that he did not perceive anything of it,—had no intimations of it? Which would the Acc. express? Why ᾐσθάνετο in the Impf.? Is the negation expressed more forcibly by the Aor. or the Impf.? Does the Impf. state simply the historic fact that he did not perceive the plot, or, stronger than that, that there was no time when he perceived it,—the Impf. denoting the continuance of the time? By what is Τισσαφέρνει governed? Rule (161, 2, a, γ)? Derivation of ἐνόμιζε? Of νόμος? From what part of νέμω? Why ἐνόμιζε Impf.? Is it a mute or a liquid verb? Is its characteristic pure or impure (104, 3)? With what does πολεμοῦντα agree? Why properispomenon? Derivation? What relation does it express, that of *manner*, *means*, or *cause* (176, 1)? What part of speech, which the Greek has not, would the Latin use instead of it?[59] On what does δαπανᾶν depend? Its subject? Construction of οὐδέν (159, 7, and R)? Composition? Is it according to rule or exception that the δ

αὐτῶν πολεμούντων· καὶ γὰρ ὁ Κῦρος ἀπέπεμπε τοὺς γιγνομένους δασμοὺς βασιλεῖ ἐκ τῶν πόλεων ὧν ὁ Τισσαφέρνης ἐτύγχανεν ἔχων. Ἄλλο δὲ στράτευμα

before the aspirate ἐν is not changed into ϑ? Is the explanation of the Impf. ἤχϑετο the same as that of ᾐσϑάνετο above? Fut. of ἤχϑετο? How is the ε before the σ to be explained? Construction of αὐτῶν? Is it the Gen. absolute or the causal Gen. depending on ἤχϑετο (158, 6, I)? What case does ἤχϑετο more commonly take? Would a subordinate clause introduced by ὅτι be equivalent to αὐτῶν πολεμούντων? Force of καί before γάρ? Does the English ordinarily translate it in such cases? Does the use of it in Greek, however, make the connection between the sentences more or less close than in the English? Why ἀπέπεμπε active? Why Impf.? Does it denote what was done once, or what was regularly done, from time to time? Meaning of γιγνομένους here? What is the syllable γι? What vowel of the root does that syllable reject? Derivation of δασμούς? What does ἐκ show the relation between? Why the article with πόλεων? What expression makes it definite? What peculiarity in the accent? How to be explained (46)? By what principle is ὧν in the Gen? Is it proper to give a rule for its government as a Gen.? In what case would it regularly have been (182, 6)? Such attractions occur generally only with verbs governing what case?[60] Stem of ἐτύγχανεν? How from that stem is the Pres. τυγχάνω formed? What relation does ἔχων sustain to ἐτύγχανεν (175, 3)?

By what principle is αὐτῷ in the Dat.? Is it the Dat.

αὐτῷ συνελέγετο ἐν Χεῤῥονήσῳ τῇ καταντιπέρας Ἀβύδου τόνδε τὸν τρόπον. Κλέαρχος Λακεδαιμόνιος φυγὰς ἦν· τούτῳ συγγενόμενος ὁ Κῦρος ἠγάσθη τε αὐτὸν

of the agent (*was collected by him*), or the limiting Dat. (*was collected for him*)? Only what parts of the verb generally take the Dat. of the agent?[61] Composition of Χεῤῥονήσου? How else is the word written?[62] Literal meaning? With what English word does it nearly correspond in meaning? What Chersonese is meant? What determines that? Where was it? When the people of Athens spoke of it, did they connect any epithet with it, or define it at all, or simply speak of *the Chersonese*? How, then, would it be known what one was meant? Why the article τῇ after Χεῤῥονήσῳ? It shows that καταντιπέρας Ἀβύδου sustains what relation to Χεῤῥονήσῳ? How else could τῇ .... Ἀβύδου be placed to have the same force as at present?[63] Construction of Ἀβύδου (158, R. 1, d)? Where was Abydus? Was it on the Asiatic or European side of the Hellespont? Force of δε in τόνδε (64, 3)? Derivation of τρόπον? From what part of that verb? Construction? Is it governed by anything? Is it a kind of adverbial expression? How does it differ from τροπόν? Who was Clearchus? What was his history up to this time? Derivation of φυγάς? Stem? Why does not the δ appear in the Nom? Declension? What kind of a passive is ἠγάσθη (118, R.; 144, b, and R)? The passive, then, has the force of what voice? Does the Aor. of this word denote merely a past act (*he esteemed him*), or the coming into a state or condition (*he came to esteem*

καὶ δίδωσιν αὐτῷ μυρίους δαρεικούς. Ὁ δὲ λαβὼν τὸ χρυσίον στράτευμα συνέλεξεν ἀπὸ τούτων τῶν χρημάτων καὶ ἐπολέμει ἐκ Χεῤῥονήσου ὁρμώμενος τοῖς Θρᾳξὶ τοῖς ὑπὲρ Ἑλλήσποντον οἰκοῦσι, καὶ ὠφέλει

him)? (Compare ἐβασίλευσα, not *I was a king*, but *I came to be a king*.) Force of τε before αὐτόν? What is its correlative? Could τε be omitted? Would anything be lost by the omission? What kind of a Pres. is δίδωσιν? What is the advantage of a present over a past tense here? Different accentuation of μυριοι? Which accent makes it mean a definite number (ten thousand), and which an indefinite? Is this distinction always observed, however? Derivation of δαρεικούς? How much was a Daric? Any peculiarity in the use of ὁ here? Any other instances of a similar usage in this chapter? Rule for the accent of λαβών (84, 3, a)? What relation of time does it sustain to συνέλεξεν? Why the article with χρυσίον? Derivation of χρημάτων? From what part of that verb? From what person of that tense? Why ἐπολέμει Impf.? How does ἐκ Χεῤῥονήσου differ from ἀπὸ Χεῤῥονήσου? Which would necessarily imply that the person spoken of was *in* the place, and which might only imply that he was *on the borders*? Why ὁρμώμενος in the Mid. voice? Difference between it and active? Is the Act., however, often used intransitively? Force of the present Part.? Does the Pres. or Past Part. denote the repetition of the act? Construction of Θρᾳξί (161, 2, a, γ)? Why the article repeated after it? What relation does it make ὑπὲρ Ἑλλήσποντον sus-

τοὺς Ἕλληνας· ὥστε καὶ χρήματα συνεβάλλοντο αὐτῷ εἰς τὴν τροφὴν τῶν στρατιωτῶν αἱ Ἑλλησποντιακαὶ πόλεις ἑκοῦσαι. Τοῦτο δ' αὖ οὕτω τρεφόμενον ἐλάν-

tain to Θρᾳξί? How else could ὑπὲρ . . . οἰκοῦσι be placed to have the same force?[63] Composition of Ἑλλήσποντον? Why so called? Is οἰκοῦσι a verb or a participle? Is there any difference in form or accent? How determined, then? Tense of ὠφέλει? How determined whether it is Pres. or Impf.? Are the form and accent the same in both tenses? Which is alike, and which different? What is the difference? What case do verbs of the signification of ὠφέλει govern in Latin (159, 3)? Why the article with Ἕλληνας? Does it make the word denote some particular Greeks, or Greeks in general? Force of καί after ὥστε? Influence of συν in συνεβάλλοντο? Why Impf.? How much of the word exhibits the active form? What is -το? Why the Mid. voice? Whose money do they bring together or contribute? Construction of αὐτῷ? What does εἰς show the relation between? What relation does εἰς τὴν τροφήν sustain to αὐτῷ? Which is the general, and which the specific expression? How can the sentence be translated to denote these relations respectively?[64] Derivation of τροφήν? From what part of the verb? Declension of στρατιωτῶν? On what principle perispomenon (26, 4, γ)? Accent of Nom. Sing.? Voc. Sing.? Why not the Voc. like the Nom.? How is the syllable ου in ἑκοῦσαι to be explained? What two letters are dropped? Why (8, 8)? On what principle does ο become ου after these letters are dropped? Why are πόλεις ἑκοῦσαι placed at the end of

θανεν αὐτῷ τὸ στράτευμα. Ἀρίστιππος δὲ ὁ Θετταλὸς ξένος ὢν ἐτύγχανεν αὐτῷ, καὶ πιεζόμενος ὑπὸ τῶν οἴκοι ἀντιστασιωτῶν ἔρχεται πρὸς τὸν Κῦρον καὶ αἰτεῖ αὐτὸν εἰς δισχιλίους ξένους καὶ τριῶν μηνῶν μισθόν, ὡς οὕτω

the sentence? Is στράτευμα for the same reason placed at the end of the next sentence? How is the participle connected with λανθάνω to be translated, as a participle or verb? How is λανθάνω to be translated, as a verb or adverb (175, 3)? Fut. of τρέφω? On what principle is τ changed into θ in the Fut. (8, 10)? Stem of ἐλάνθανεν? How from the stem λαθ is the Pres. λανθάνω formed (121, b)? Who was Aristippus? Where was Thessaly, to which he belonged? Construction of ξένος? Is it the predicate Nom. after ὤν or ἐτύγχανεν? What relation does ὤν sustain to ἐτύγχανεν? Is ὑπό the usual preposition with a passive verb to denote the voluntary agent? What Latin preposition would be here used, instead of ὑπό? Why is not οἴκοι properispomenon? What two methods of explaining this?[65] How does οἶκοι differ in meaning from οἴκοι? Case of οἴκοι? Composition of ἀντιστασιωτῶν? Why perispomenon? Fut. of ἔρχεται for Attic Greek (126, 2)? From what stem is the Perf. formed? What peculiarity has the Perf. (89)? Verbs of asking, as αἰτεῖ, govern two accusatives, — what are they here? Is ξένους governed by εἰς or αἰτεῖ?[66] Why μηνῶν accented on the ultimate (33, III, b)? Why circumflexed? Construction of μισθόν? Whose view is indicated by ὡς with the participle, — that of the writer or Aristippus

περιγενόμενος ἂν τῶν ἀντιστασιωτῶν. Ὁ δὲ Κῦρος δίδωσιν αὐτῷ εἰς τετρακισχιλίους καὶ ἓξ μηνῶν μισθὸν, καὶ δεῖται αὐτοῦ μὴ πρόσθεν καταλῦσαι πρὸς τοὺς

(176, R. 2)? How may the force of ὡς be expressed?[46] How much of what precedes does οὕτω embrace, or to what does it refer? What part of a proposition is contained in it (185, R. 4)? How can it be expressed as part of a proposition?[67] What part of a proposition is περιγενόμενος ἄν? What effect has ἄν on the participle here?[68] When may ἄν stand with the participle (153, 2, d)? How could οὕτω περιγενόμενος ἄν be expressed in the form of a regular protasis and apodosis? By what principle is ἀντιστασιωτῶν in the Gen. (158, 7, *a*)? Δίδωσιν, being a transitive verb, requires its direct object in the Acc., — what is that Acc. here? Is it τετρακισχιλίους? But is not this governed by εἰς? What then is the grammatical object of δίδωσιν? What does καί before ἕξ connect? Has δεῖται here its primary or secondary meaning? What is its meaning here? Is it a contract verb in all its parts? In what only (97, 1)? Construction of αὐτοῦ (158, 5, a)? Why μή here and not οὐ? General difference between these words (177, 3, 4, and 5)? Which is joined almost always with the Inf.? With what Latin words do πρόσθεν .... πρίν correspond? Meaning of καταλῦσαι? How much is simple stem? What is the σ? From the circumflex on the penult what is to be inferred in regard to the quantity of the ultimate, so far as relates to accent? On what kind of a syllable only can the circumflex stand? Can an acute accent stand either on a

ἀντιστασιώτας πρὶν ἂν αὐτῷ συμβουλεύσηται. Οὕτω δὲ αὖ τὸ ἐν Θετταλίᾳ ἐλάνθανεν αὐτῷ τρεφόμενον στράτευμα. Πρόξενον δὲ τὸν Βοιώτιον, ξένον ὄντα αὐτῷ, ἐκέλευσε λαβόντα ἄνδρας ὅτι πλείστους παραγενέσθαι,

long or a short syllable? From the acute on the penult of ἀντιστασιώτας, what may be inferred in regard to the quantity of the ultimate? If it were not so, and the accent were on the penult, what would the accent be? Is -ας in the ending of nouns of the third Dec. long or short (31)? Why συμβουλεύσηται in the Mid. voice? What relation of time does it express (152, R. 3)? What relation of future time, — simple Fut. or Fut. Perf.? What is implied by a Fut. Perf.? A Fut. Perf. being really a future Past, which is a contradiction, can there be *absolutely* a Fut. Perf.? How is the expression, *Future Perfect*, then, to be understood, as an absolute or a relative term? What relation does the time of συμβουλεύσηται sustain to that of καταλῦσαι? Do they both denote future time? Which is prior to the other? Construction of ξένον? What relation does ὄντα express, — time, cause, or conditionality (176)? Primary meaning of ἐκέλευσε? Is Πρόξενον governed by ἐκέλευσε, or is it the subject Acc. before παραγενέσθαι?[69] Rule for accentuation of παραγενέσθαι? Of λαβόντα? Were the written accents, as they now stand on the Greek words, used in the best period of the language? About how early were they introduced? What occasion was there for them then more than previously?[70] Meaning of ὡς before εἰς Πεισίδας? Does it mean "saying that,"

ὡς εἰς Πεισίδας βουλόμενος στρατεύεσθαι, ὡς πράγματα παρεχόντων τῶν Πεισιδῶν τῇ ἑαυτοῦ χώρᾳ. Σοφαίνετον δὲ τὸν Στυμφάλιον καὶ Σωκράτην τὸν Ἀχαιόν, ξένους ὄντας καὶ τούτους, ἐκέλευσεν ἄνδρας λαβόντας

"on the pretence that," or what? If it were omitted, what different sense would the sentence have? Where was Pisidia? Derivation of *στρατεύεσθαι*? Does *ὡς* before *πράγματα* have the same meaning as the one before *εἰς*? Derivation of *πράγματα*? From what part of *πράττω*? What person of the Perf. Pass.? What noun comes from the second Pers.? What from the third? Has *πράγματα* here its usual meaning? What is its meaning here? Composition of *ἑαυτοῦ*? What other form can it have? What is the position of the Gen. of reflexive pronouns with reference to the substantive on which they depend? Could *ἑαυτοῦ* be placed before the article *τῇ*, or immediately after *χώρᾳ*? Would the position *τῇ χώρᾳ τῇ ἑαυτοῦ* have the same force as that in the text (148, R. 8)? If instead of *ἑαυτοῦ* in the text, we have a simple personal pronoun, *μοῦ*, *σοῦ*, *ἡμῶν*, *αὐτοῦ*, etc., how would it be placed? How would the demonstrative *τούτου* be placed, — like *ἑαυτοῦ* or *ἐμοῦ*, etc.?[71] In transferring Greek proper names into English, how is *οι*, as in *Βοιώτιον*, expressed? How *αι*, as in *Σοφαίνετον* (3, R. 1)? Force of *καί* before *τούτους*? Upon what word does its force fall? To what previous word does it direct the mind? From what Pres. does *ἐλθεῖν* come? From what root? What letter is syncopated in the form? Rule for accent (84, 3, a)? Pecu-

ἐλθεῖν ὅτι πλείστους, ὡς πολεμήσων Τισσαφέρνει σὺν τοῖς φυγάσι τῶν Μιλησίων. Καὶ ἐποίουν οὕτως οὗτοι.

liarity of the Perf.? Force of ὅτι before πλείστους? What is denoted by the Fut. Part. πολεμήσων? Construction of Τισσαφέρνει? Does σύν govern more than one case? What letter is dropped in φυγάσι? Why? How is φυγάσι accented in the Nom.? Can any rules be given by which the place of the accent may be determined? How are such rules obtained? In any other way than by observation, grouping together words similarly accented in classes, under a general rule?[72] With a few exceptions, is the place of the accent uniform in the verb? What is that place? Does σύν here have the meaning of the English *with*, as when we say, "England is going to war *with* France," or does it mean, "in conjunction with," "with the aid of"? Μιλησίων being formed from the noun Μίλητος, by the influence of what letter is the τ changed into σ?[73] Why the Impf. ἐποίουν? Does it mean they wished, they endeavored (152, R. 4) to do it, or they went to doing it? The writer might have used the Aor. here, but what would have been the difference in the view given (152, 10)? Derivation of οὕτως? What is the usage of the Greek by which οὕτως οὗτοι are placed together?[74]

HOMER.

QUESTIONS ON THE FIRST THIRTY-TWO LINES OF THE ILIAD.

Why is this poem called the Iliad? Is it definitely known when it was composed? How early was it known in European Greece?[1] Was the author a European or Asiatic Greek? Who was the author? Has there been any doubt in regard to the authorship? Can anything be ascertained of the personal history of Homer from his own writings? Was he probably born blind? Is it known when he lived? How many cities claimed to have been his birth-place? What two places are generally regarded as having the strongest claim? Was the poem probably committed to writing by the author? Was writing known in the time of Homer? Who first collected the poems of Homer in the form we now have them? Was the Iliad originally divided into twenty-four books, as at present? How then were the different parts designated? What is the meaning of Λοιμός, Μῆνις, at the commencement of the first book, and other inscriptions at the commencement of the other books?[2] What is the dialect of Homer, — is it the older or the later Ionic, or neither? General characteristics of the Ionic dialect? Why called Ionic? Where used principally? What is the subjec

MHNIN ἄειδε, θεά, Πηληϊάδεω Ἀχιλῆος

of the poem? Who is the hero? Why does not the author commence with an account of the circumstances which led to the disagreement between Achilles and Agamemnon, instead of reserving this account for the 365 line, *et seq.*? Would the effect have been as impressive, if the poet had given these circumstances in a narrative form, as they are coming from the lips of Achilles himself?

Why does μῆνιν stand as the first word? Derivation? If from μένω, what is its precise meaning? If from μαίνομαι, what? Any other form of the Acc. besides μῆνιν? What was the method of reciting verse which makes the use of ἄειδε proper?[3] Prose form instead of ἄειδε? Fut. of ἀείδω? Of ᾄδω? Who is the θεά invoked? Was it any divinity known by name to the poet, or simply the Muse of Epic poetry? How is θεά, *goddess*, distinguished from the same form meaning *sight*? What kind of a noun is Πηληϊάδεω? From what noun is the patronymic formed? Meaning of patronymics? What other patronymics could be formed from Πηλεύς (Comp. lines 188 and 223)? When does the patronymic end in -ιάδης? Why -ιάδης when the final vowel of the stem is long? Why not -ίδης as well? Could such a form as Πηληΐδης be introduced into hexameter verse? Why not? What are the Gen. Sing. endings of masculine nouns of the first Dec., in Homer (197, 4)? How from the Gen. in -αο come the forms in -ω and -εω? Do the vowels -εω in Πηληϊάδεω form two syllables? What is the figure called by which they are

Οὐλομένην, ἣ μυρί' Ἀχαιοῖς ἄλγε' ἔθηκεν,
Πολλὰς δ' ἰφθίμους ψυχὰς Ἄϊδι προΐαψεν

pronounced as one syllable (194, 4)? How can the accent be upon the antepenult when the ultimate is long (30, R. 2)? Gen. Sing. of Πηληϊάδεω in Attic? Is the Gen. ending -ου ever found in Homer in masculine nouns of the first Dec.? In what three respects does the Gen. Ἀχιλῆος differ in form from the Attic Gen.? Why one λ dropped? Why ε of the Attic η here? How is the Attic Gen. accented? Derivation of οὐλομένην? Has it an active or a passive sense? How is the syllable οὐ explained? Before what letters may ο be lengthened into ου?[4] What instance in the tenth line? Antecedent of ἥ? How is μυριοι accented when it means *ten thousand*? How when it denotes an indefinite number? Is this distinction uniformly observed? Has the word here its specific or indefinite sense? Who were the Ἀχαιοί? Why does Homer use this word, instead of some other, to designate Greeks? Why not Ἕλλησι? Which would an Attic writer use? Full form instead of ἄλγε'? Is the termination -εα usually contracted in Homer?[5] The measure would have been the same if the full form ἄλγεα had been retained, and the augment of ἔθηκεν omitted, — would the rhythm have been as good? What caesura is secured by the form ἄλγε' that would be lost if the full form was written?[6] Is the Dual and Pl. of ἔθηκεν used? How is its place supplied (131, 2)? What peculiarity does ἔθηκεν present in the first Aor.? What other Aorists have the same (131, 2)? What is the origin of the final ν in ἔθηκεν? Is it a para-

Ἡρώων, αὐτοὺς δὲ ἑλώρια τεῦχε κύνεσσιν

gogic ν, or does it belong to the original and full form of the word?[7] In what number, genders, and cases is πόλλας irregular in its inflection? Form of Nom. in Attic? Two forms of Nom. in Homer (201, 3)? Derivation of ἰφθίμους? Is it a compound? Gender? How can it be feminine? Does it belong appropriately to ψυχάς or ἡρώων? What is the quantity of -ας final in the Acc. Pl. of the first Dec. (25)? Of the third (31)? Composition of Ἄϊδι? Construction? Nom.? But can this come from the form Ἀΐδης? To what assumed Nom. must Ἄϊδι be referred? What is the figure by which different forms like Ἀΐδαο, Ἄιδος, Ἄϊδι (first and third Dec.) are referred to the same Nom.?[8] Force of προ in προΐαψεν? Does προΐαψεν take the augment here or not? How is that determined? If it had the augment would the ι be long or short (86)? Which is it? What are the elements of the ψ? With what is αὐτούς contrasted? What then does αὐτούς mean? How is the hiatus after δέ to be accounted for? What character or letter originally preceded the ἑ of ἑλώρια (193)? Would there, then, be any hiatus (191, g)? Construction of αὐτούς and ἑλώρια (160, 3)? Derivation of ἑλώρια? Why is not its final vowel elided, and the augment of τεῦχε retained, as in ἔθηκεν above? What caesura would there then be in the fourth foot? Was that a favorite one with Homer, or was it avoided?[9] If the augment of τεῦχε were used, how would the word be accented? Why τεῦχε Impf., while ἔθηκεν and προΐαψεν are in the Aor.? Was the distinction between the Impf.

Οἰωνοῖσί τε πᾶσι — Διὸς δ' ἐτελείετο βουλή —

and Aor. as clearly marked in Homer's time as subsequently? May he not, too, even where the action is momentary, and consequently requires an Aor., use the Impf. to denote that the effects of the action continue? Nom. Sing. of κύνεσσιν? What letter of the stem is dropped in the oblique cases? What is its Dat. Pl. in Attic? Epic endings of Dat. Pl. (199, 1)? When one and when two σ's? Why does the poet speak of giving their bodies to *dogs* and *birds of prey*? Was there anything particularly harrowing to the mind of a Greek in such a thought? Why? Attic Dat. of οἰωνοῖσι? Derivation? What, then, is the primary idea? What kind of birds are denoted? In what other sense is οἰωνός often used? What is noticeable in the position of τε standing after οἰωνοῖσι?[10] Meaning of πᾶσι here? From what assumed Nom. is Διός formed? With what Nom. is it associated? Why oxytone? Is the δ' after Διός adversative or continuative? If adversative, what is the clause with which it stands in contrast? *Notwithstanding what*, was the will of Zeus accomplishing? Why is the ε of δέ not retained, and the augment of ἐτελείετο dropped? What caesura would that give? From what Pres. does Homer form ἐτελείετο? What is the Attic Pres.? Attic Impf.? Why Mid. voice? Force of Impf.? How was the will of Zeus accomplishing? What was that will or purpose? If it was his purpose to give success to the Greeks, how are these woes that are now befalling them, to be explained? Accent of βουλή in Gen. Sing.? Nom. Pl.?

Ἐξ οὗ δὴ ταπρῶτα διαστήτην ἐρίσαντε
Ἀτρείδης τε ἄναξ ἀνδρῶν καὶ δῖος Ἀχιλλεύς.

Does ἐξ οὗ depend on ἄλγε' ἔθηκεν, προΐαψεν, etc., or ἐτελείετο βουλή? Why ἐξ, and not ἐκ? What would be the full expression instead of ἐξ οὗ?[11] Force of δή here? To what class of words does it give explicitness, or a determinate force?[12] What word does it affect? Derivation of πρῶτα? Literal meaning of διαστήτην? Force of δια? In what number is the verb? Why? Is the Dual always used when two persons or things are spoken of (147, R. 3)? Why is the augment omitted? Would the monotony of three successive *e* sounds be preferable to the present form? Which Aor. is διαστήτην? Difference between the first and second Aor. of ἵστημι (131, R. 2)? Difference between the second Aor. Act. and Mid.? Is the second Aor. Mid. in use? Why not? Derivation of ἐρίσαντε? Agreement? What relation does it express (176)? Cause of what action? How is the patronymic Ἀτρείδης formed? What other forms could be given? Force of τε after Ἀτρείδης? Could it be omitted? Without changing the sentence in any way? Stem of ἄναξ? How from the stem is the Nom. formed? What letter is appended to the stem? What is that letter? What letter of the stem does it reject? How is the ξ formed? Two forms of the Voc. Sing.? When one and when the other used? Why is not the ε in τε elided before ἄναξ? Is there not a hiatus occasioned by retaining it? What prevented the hiatus? What character or letter belonged to ἄναξ which would obviate the hiatus? Stem of ἀνδρῶν? What becomes of

Τίς τ' ἄρ σφωε θεῶν ἔριδι ξυνέηκε μάχεσθαι;
Λητοῦς καὶ Διὸς υἱός. ὁ γὰρ βασιλῆϊ χολωθεὶς

the ε? In what cases only is it retained? How does the ι in δῖος become long? What is the uncontracted form? Force of τε after τίς?[13] What is the usual position of τε with reference to the word it connects? What connection does ἄρ (ἄρα) mark with what precedes? Number of σφωε? To whom referring? Why without an accent? When the accent of an enclitic unites with the preceding oxytone, on what principle does the accent which would otherwise be depressed, become acute?[14] What Greek verb from ἔριδι? Is ἔριδι an adjunct of ξυνέηκε or μάχεσθαι? Can this be definitely determined? Why not? Does Homer connect it with words of both significations? Is ξύν or σύν the earlier form? How is the ε before the η in ξυνέηκε to be explained? What other peculiarity does this Aor. form present (Comp. ἔθηκεν above)? What is the Epic Fut. of μάχεσθαι? Attic? How is each formed? What relation has the next half line to the preceding line? Nom. of Λητοῦς? How declined, and why so accented (43, b)? Construction of υἱός? How accented in the Gen. and Dat.? Peculiarity in the use of ὁ as compared with Attic Greek? What was the original use of the Attic article, — did it have the relation of an article or pronoun? What would an Attic writer use for ὁ here? Composition of γάρ? Connection between the sentence commencing ὁ γάρ, etc., and what precedes? Attic form and accent instead of βασιλῆϊ? Who is meant by it? Construction [161, 2, (c), (β)]? To whom does ὁ refer?

Νοῦσον ἀνὰ στρατὸν ὦρσε κακήν, ὀλέκοντο δὲ λαοί,
Οὕνεκα τὸν Χρύσην ἠτίμησ' ἀρητῆρα

Why was he angry with the king? Derivation and primary meaning of χολωθείς? What English word from that noun? What connection between the primary meaning of the noun and that of the Part. here? How does the syllable -είς in χολωθείς originate? Common form instead of νοῦσον? By what general usage in Homer is the ο lengthened into ου? Primary meaning of ἀνά? Meaning here? How comes such a meaning from the primary one? Stem of ὦρσε? What syllable is added to the stem to form the Pres.? When is νυ and when ννυ added? Is it usual for liquid verbs to form the Fut. or first Aor. with σ? Peculiarity in the Perf. of ὦρσε? How is κακός compared in Homer (202, 2)? What peculiarity in ὀλέκοντο? What is the general rule in regard to the omission of the augment in Homer (205, 1)? Will that determine every case (Comp. ἔθηκεν and τεῦχε above)? Only what tenses of ὀλέκοντο are in use? Why Mid. voice here? Difference between Mid. and Act.? Derivation? Relation of the first half of the line to the second? Of the second to the first? Derivation of λαοί? Why so derived, — what connection have people with stones? Full form instead of οὕνεκα? By what principle does it have this form (6, 2)? Has τόν here simply the force of the Attic article, or a strictly pronominal force?[15] Who was Chryses? How had he been dishonored? Composition and derivation of ἠτίμησ'? Derivation of ἀρητῆρα? How differing from ἱερῆα, line 23? What metrical peculiarity in this (11)

10*

Ἀτρείδης. ὁ γὰρ ἦλθε θοὰς ἐπὶ νῆας Ἀχαιῶν
Λυσόμενός τε θύγατρα φέρων τ' ἀπερείσι' ἄποινα,
Στέμματ' ἔχων ἐν χερσὶν ἑκηβόλου Ἀπόλλωνος

line? What is meant by a spondaic line? Full form of ἦλθε (Comp. line 152)? Epic Fut. and Perf.? Attic? The two different significations of ἔρχομαι? Derivation of θόας? Attic for νῆας? What other Epic form besides this (200, 3; and comp. line 487)? How much of λυσόμενος is verb stem? What is the σ? Why has the word two accents? Force of the Fut. Part.? Why Mid. voice? Difference between Act. and Mid. of this verb? If a person owning a slave or captive sets him free, by which voice is the act designated? But if another person purchases him, or procures his freedom from the owner, by which voice is this act designated (Comp. λῦσαι, line 20)? The office of τέ after λυσόμενος? Where is the correlative? Is τέ .... τέ usual in Attic Greek? What is the more common formula there corresponding to τέ .... τέ here (178, 3)? Peculiarity in the form of θύγατρα (199, 7)? Why not φέρων in the Fut. as well as λυσόμενος? Did he not come for the *purpose* of bringing the ransom? But is the purpose or the *means* more prominently designated by φέρων? Fut. of φέρω? From what theme formed? Perf.? From what theme? Composition of ἀπερείσι'? What change has taken place in it? Why? Composition of ἄποινα? What Latin word from the last part of the compound? What English? Derivation of στέμμα? From what part of that word? What was the στέμμα? How worn usually? By what English

Χρυσέῳ ἀνὰ σκήπτρῳ, καὶ ἐλίσσετο πάντας Ἀχαιούς,
Ἀτρείδα δὲ μάλιστα δύω, κοσμήτορε λαῶν·
Ἀτρεῖδαί τε καὶ ἄλλοι ἐϋκνήμιδες Ἀχαιοί,

preposition may ἔχων with the Acc. be translated here, and in similar places? What is ἐν with reference to accent? On what principle is χερσίν accented on the ultimate (33, III, b.)? Is the ι of the stem omitted in any other case than the Dat. Pl.? Composition of ἑκηβόλου? From what part of the verb does βόλου come? What kind of a line is this (14) metrically? What object has the priest in taking the στέμμα of Apollo? Why upon the sceptre? Of what was the sceptre a symbol? What figure is there in the scanning of χρυσέῳ (194, 4)? How is the ω made short (190, 7)? What would be the Attic form instead of χρυσέῳ? Why the open or uncontracted form here? Does ἀνά govern the Dat. in prose? Derivation of σκήπτρῳ? Meaning of the verb? Difference between the Pres. and Fut. of λίσσομαι? Case and number of Ἀτρείδα? Why not the circumflex on the penult? Is δέ adversative or continuative? Comparative of μάλιστα? Origin of the second λ? Does the Attic use δύω? What is the Attic form? Does the Epic use any form besides δύω? Why is δύω used with the Dual Ἀτρείδα, — does not the Dual alone signify the *two* sons of Atreus? Was the distinction between the Dual and the Plural as clearly marked in Homer's time as subsequently?[16] Derivation of κοσμήτορε? And κοσμέω from what? Primary meaning of κόσμος, from which κοσμέω is derived? Why has Ἀτρεῖδαι the circumflex,

Ὑμῖν μὲν θεοὶ δοῖεν Ὀλύμπια δώματ' ἔχοντες
Ἐκπέρσαι Πριάμοιο πόλιν, εὖ δ' οἴκαδ' ἱκέσθαι·

but Ἀτρείδα the acute upon the penult? Is not the final syllable of both long in quantity? But how is -αι regarded in respect to accent (26, 4, a)? Who are the sons of Atreus here referred to? Difference between τὲ καί and καί alone? What word would an Attic writer join with ἄλλοι, which is not here? Composition of ἐϋκνήμιδες? How were the κνημῖδες made,—in one or two pieces? Why? Of what material? Does ἐϋκνήμιδες denote the whole of their armour, or is it simply a part put for the whole? What other form in Epic besides ὑμῖν (203)? What figure in the scanning of θεοί (194, 4)? In Attic Greek would θεοί take the article, or not? Did the article, as such, exist in Homer's time? Why is δοῖεν in the Opt.? What other form besides this? What is the grammatical object of δοῖεν? Why were the gods represented as dwelling on Olympus? Was there more than one mountain of this name? What one is meant here? How high is it? Derivation of δώματα? Why the acute on the ω here, while the Nom. Sing. is circumflexed? From what Pres. is ἐκπέρσαι? What has become of the θ? What letter rejects it? Rule for the accent (84, 4, a)? Attic Gen., instead of Πριάμοιο? Is the Gen. in -ου of the second Dec. found in Homer? Why called the city of Priam? Epic Gen. Sing. of πόλις (199, 16)? Force of δε appended to οἶκα? What case is οἶκα, and from what assumed Nom.? From what Pres. is ἱκέσθαι? Rule for accent (84, 4, a)? Stem? What is appended to the stem (120, 2)? Fut.

Παῖδα δ' ἐμοὶ λῦσαί τε φίλην τὰ τ' ἄποινα δέχεσθαι,
Ἁζόμενοι Διὸς υἱὸν ἑκηβόλον Ἀπόλλωνα.
Ἔνθ' ἄλλοι μὲν πάντες ἐπευφήμησαν Ἀχαιοί

how formed? Stem of παῖδα? Nom. how formed from it? Accent of Gen. and Dat. Sing.? Principle? On what does the Inf. λῦσαι depend? When it is said that it is used for the Imperative, what is meant? Was the grammatical construction as perfect in the earlier period of the language as later?[17] Why is λῦσαι properispomenon, while ἐκπέρσαι is paroxytone? Has τά here the force of an article or a pronoun? Why is λῦσαι Aor., but δέχεσθαι Pres.? Which denotes the single act, and which the continuance of the result? Primary meaning of ἁζόμενοι? What tenses in use? What other form of the Acc. besides Ἀπόλλωνα? How is that form obtained? What letter is syncopated? What absorbed?

Was the Greek originally written in capitals, or in the cursive letters such as are now used?[18] How early were the cursive letters introduced?[19] Were the words originally separated from each other by spaces, as at present, or written together without spaces? Does ἔνθα primarily denote time or place? Which here? To what word is ἄλλοι antithetic? Would the Attic use οἱ here with ἄλλοι, or not? Composition of ἐπευφήμησαν? Has it any augment? What is the principle respecting the augment in verbs beginning with εὐ (90, 2)? Derivation of αἰδεῖσθαι? Why properispomenon? What would be the accent before contraction? Do all contracted syllables which have the accent, take the circumflex [11, 2, (2), (b)]? Of what

Αἰδεῖσθαί θ' ἱερῆα καὶ ἀγλαὰ δέχθαι ἄποινα·
Ἀλλ' οὐκ Ἀτρείδῃ Ἀγαμέμνονι ἥνδανε θυμῷ,
Ἀλλὰ κακῶς ἀφίει, κρατερὸν δ' ἐπὶ μῦθον ἔτελλεν·

word is θ' the representative? How does it receive this form? Attic for ἱερῆα (199, 10)? How accented? Tense of δέχθαι? From what? On what principle does the accent of ἀλλ' disappear (12, 3)? Why Ἀγαμέμνονι in Dat. [161, 2, (c), (δ)]? Stem of ἥνδανε? How from that stem is the Pres. ἀνδάνω formed (121, b)? What is the Fut.? Is it formed from the simple stem ἁδ? What letter is assumed in order to form the Fut., and why? Construction of θυμῷ? Is it in any way governed by ἥνδανε? What relation does it sustain to Ἀγαμέμνονι? Is it indispensable to the sense here? Why used then? How is κακῶς compared as an adverb (54, 1)? Why is the comparative in the singular, but the superlative in the plural? In the comparative, how many things are brought into view? More than two? As one is, therefore, compared with the other, in what number must the comparative be? In the superlative is two or more things brought into view? What, then, must be the number of the superlative? Where is ἀφίει made? From what Pres.? How this form from ἄφιημι (Comp. Impf. of τίθημι)? How can the ι in ἀφίει be short? To what word does ἐπί belong? What is the figure called by which it is separated? What is the derivation and meaning of the term *Tmesis?* What English word from μῦθον? Perf. Act. of τέλλω? How is the α in the penult of the Perf. to be

Μή σε, γέρον, κοίλῃσιν ἐγὼ παρὰ νηυσὶ κιχείω
Ἢ νῦν δηθύνοντ' ἢ ὕστερον αὖτις ἰόντα,

explained (102, 3)? In what two ways does the Fut. Act. of τέλλω differ from the Pres.?

Do the general laws of scanning apply to the Greek the same as to the Latin? In scanning Greek, is a final vowel before another word beginning with a vowel to be omitted, as in Latin (Comp. lines 4 and seven)? Are all the elisions made in the composition of Greek poetry which are intended? Was hiatus, *i. e.*, one word ending with a vowel and the next beginning with a vowel, to any extent allowed in Greek poetry? Does it occur in Greek more or less frequently than in Latin?[20] Can the quantity of the vowels be determined more easily in Greek or Latin? Why? How many of the Greek vowels determine their quantity by the form? What are they? Is this true of any of the vowels in Latin? Only how many vowels in Greek, then, do not determine the quantity by the form? Are not even these, however, when standing before another vowel, or a single consonant, in most cases short? How many times are these vowels long, except before two consonants or a double consonant, in the first twenty-five lines of the Iliad, and how many times short?

Why μή and not οὐ before σε (177, 5)? Is γέρον the pure stem, or is it shortened (35)? Nom.? By what principle is ο of the stem lengthened into ω in the Nom.?[21] Attic form for κοίλῃσιν? What other form in Epic (197, 6)? Why is the term used at all,—are not all ships hollow? Do we speak of hollow ships? Why not? Attic

Μή νύ τοι οὐ χραίσμῃ σκῆπτρον καὶ στέμμα θεοῖο.
Τὴν δ' ἐγὼ οὐ λύσω, πρίν μιν καὶ γῆρας ἔπεισιν
Ἡμετέρῳ ἐνὶ οἴκῳ, ἐν Ἄργεϊ, τηλόθι πάτρης,

for νηυσί? What two other Epic forms (200, 3)? Peculiarity in the form of κιχείω (209, 6)? Derivation of ὕστερον? How compared? What influence has it on αὖτις, — does it weaken or strengthen it? From what is αὖτις formed? Its Attic form? Is ἰόντα a Pres. or second Aor. Part.? Is its accent, however, that of a Pres. or Aor.? Attic for τοί? What other Epic form (203)? Tense of χραίσμῃ? Is the Pres. in use? Attic word for τήν? Was the Attic or Ionic the earlier dialect? Why called Attic? Was it confined to Attica? When did the Attic supersede the Ionic?[22] Why οὐ and not μή with λύσω? Why λύσω in Act.? What is the Stem? σ? ω? Peculiarity of μιν? How many genders does it represent? Construction?[23] Does καί mean *also* or *even*? How determined? On what word does its force fall? Has ἔπεισιν a Pres. or Fut. sense (137, R. 3)? On what principle is hiatus admissible after ἡμετέρῳ and οἴκῳ (191, a)? How the one after ἐνί? What letter originally preceded οἴκῳ, which would prevent hiatus (191, g)? Attic instead of ἐνί? Why need ἐν Ἄργεϊ and τηλόθι πάτρης be introduced after he had mentioned ἡμετέρῳ ἐνὶ οἴκῳ? Did not the priest know that Agamemnon's home was in Argos, and that it was far away from Troy? But would the impression be as strong, though the facts were known, if the four last words of the line were omitted? Where was Argos? Does the word here

Ἱστὸν ἐποιχομένην καὶ ἐμὸν λέχος ἀντιόωσαν·
Ἀλλ' ἴθι, μή μ' ἐρέθιζε, σαώτερος ὥς κε νέηαι!

denote merely the city of that name? In what different senses is it used? Construction of πάτρης (157)? Attic form? What does Homer use instead of long α in the first Dec. (197, 1)? Derivation of ἱστόν? The pertinence of the name? What was the position of their web, — perpendicular or horizontal? Construction of ἱστόν? Would good prose allow so loose a construction? Agreement of ἐποιχομένην? Literal meaning? How would the two words be translated into English? Derivation of λέχος? Agreement of ἀντιόωσαν? Regular contracted form? Are the open or uncontracted forms of verbs in -άω frequent in Homer?[24] What kind of a form is this? On what principle is the resolution here made by ο (Comp. λαμπετόωντι, line 104)?[25] Derivation of ἐρέθιζε? Why σαώτερος and not σαότερος? Why is the comparative used here? What thought is suppressed which is necessary to complete the comparison, — safer than what? Does ὡς in its sense here, take an accent? Whence comes its accent, then? Difference between ὡς with and without the accent? Attic for κε? What letter is syncopated in νέηαι? Attic instead of it? How formed from this?[26]

Is the proportion of vowels here greater or less than in prose? Why so? In the first seven lines of the Iliad do the vowels or consonants predominate? In what proportion? How is it in the first seven of the Aeneid? Does that predominance of consonants over the vowels hold generally in the Latin?[27] In Greek what is the proportion of vowels to consonants?[28] How many diphthongs in the first seven lines of the Aeneid? How many in the same of the Iliad? Does that indicate the relative number in the two languages?[29] Is aspiration, as in ᾗ, ἡρώων, ἑλώρια, etc., above, more common in Greek or in Latin? How many instances of aspiration in the first twenty-five lines of the Iliad. and how many in the same of the Aeneid?

NOTES.

NOTES.

NOTES TO QUESTIONS ON THE FABLES.

1. The case-endings of Latin nouns, etc., generally denote the *relations* which the nouns, etc., express; but as the English nouns have no such case-endings, except the possessive, the relation which the Latin expresses by these endings is usually denoted in English by prepositions. Hence, to denote the relation of the Abl. *metu*, we use *by* or *from*, and for that of *milvii*, *of:* Hence, milv*ii* met*u*, *by* fear *of* the kite.

2. The rule means that, when the relation of *cause*, *manner*, or *means* is to be expressed, such relation is denoted by putting the noun in the Abl. The word, therefore, is not governed by any other word.

3. The *e* in *accipitrem*, and in all similar Accusatives of the third Dec. is a connecting vowel, connecting the stem *accipitr* with the case-ending *m*. The *e* of the Nom. is dropped in the oblique cases.

4. The proper root of *rogo* is *roga*, contraction taking place in the Pres., as *rogao*, *rogo*, *rogaas*, *rogas*, etc. The grammar, however, to which references are made in these "Questions," does not adopt this explanation.

5. The *dentals* (or *linguals*) *d* and *t* are either dropped before *s*, to soften the pronunciation, as (claudsi) *clausi*, (ridsi) *risi*, (sentsi) *sensi*, (dividsum) *divisum*, etc.; or they are assimilated before *s*, as *cessi* for *cedsi*.

6. The Latin has no substantive personal pronoun of the third person; *ille hic*, *is*, etc., are not properly substantive personal pronouns,

with the meaning of *he*, etc., but demonstrative *adjective* pronouns agreeing with some noun understood. They are, however, quite frequently used as personal pronouns.

7. All ablatives Sing. of the fifth Dec. are formed by contraction, *ee* being contracted into *ē*, as diee, *diē*. This declension, like the fourth, is but a modification of the third.

8. Twenty-three simple verbs in Latin have the reduplication, — two of the first conjugation, four of the second, and seventeen of the third.

9. The clause following *quam* completes the comparison which was commenced in the preceding clause by *majorem*, — the comparison being imperfect without the clause with *quam*.

10. The form of the Nom. of the third Dec. generally differs from the stem or root; but the stem may be found by rejecting *is* of the Gen. Sing., as tempor*is*, stem *tempor*; civitat*is*, stem *civitat*.

11. *Potuisset* is strictly the apodosis of a proposition, the protasis being understood, such as "had he made the trial." (See Gram. 261, R. 4.)

12. There is only a connection of *signification* between *malus* and the comparative and superlative, — none in form; the comparative and superlative in use supply those of *malus* which are not in use.

13. The *m* of *com* and *n* of *in* are assimilated before liquids, as *irruo* (*inruo*), *corruo* (*conruo*), *illĭno* (*inlino*), etc. (See Gram. 196, 5.)

14. The Latin has no Perf. Act. Participle, as the English; therefore it cannot have a construction like the English, "having gnawed the nets," and the like.

15. The relative at the commencement of a sentence generally differs from the demonstratives *hic* or *ille*, in having a *connective* force. The connective force may be expressed in various ways, as *now*, *then*, and the like.

16. When the action denoted by the Abl. absolute is performed by the same agent as that denoted by the verb of the same sentence, the Perf. Pass. Part. in the Abl. absolute may be translated into

English by our Perf. Act. Part., as *recuperato gladio,* ad suos reversus est, "having recovered his sword, he returned to his party."

17. Most masculine and feminine nouns of the third Dec in the Nom. append the letter *s* to the stem; this letter is called the sign of the Nom. or the gender sign.

18. As the combination *rs* at the end of a word was not euphonic to a Roman ear, the *s* rejects the *r*, so that we have the Nom. *mus* rather than *murs*. It is sometimes said, however, that the *s* in *mus* is not the sign of the Nom., but that it stands for *r*, these letters being often interchangeable.

19. The *d* of *ad* is assimilated before *c*, *q*, *qu*, *p*, *f*, *t*, *l*, *r*, *s*.

20. The prefix *ob* was originally *obs* (obstendo), but the *b* is dropped when the prefix comes before *t*, — the combination of three consonants generally not being admissible. On the same principle the *b* of *abs* is dropped, as *aspello* for *abspello.*

21. The difference between *quis* and *qui* as an interrogative is, that *quis* inquires for the *name* of the person or thing, but *qui* for the *character* or *quality.*

22. The Perf. Act. of *sto* is irregular, both in following the analogy of the third conjugation, and in having the reduplication. If the Perf. were formed regularly it would be *stavi.* In the Perf. *steti* it will also be observed that the *s* of the stem syllable is omitted before *t;* hence *steti* for *stesti.* The same occurs in *spopondi* for *spospondi,* and in other words, the repetition of the *s* being uneuphonic.

23. Where the vowel of the stem is changed in the Perf. the vowel of reduplication is *e*, as sto (stem, stao), *steti;* do (stem, dao), *dedi;* parco, *peperci;* cado, *cecĭdi.* Where *e* belongs to the stem it is retained in the reduplication, as tendo, *tetendi;* pello, *pepuli.* So, too, other vowels are retained where the root is not changed, as curro, *cucurri;* spondeo, *spopondi.*

24. In the verb *eo* the *e* remains before a vowel, but is changed into *i* before a consonant. But in the Pres. Part. (*iens*), *i* stands before a vowel.

25. Some nouns of the third Dec., whose stem ends in *n*, omit the Nom. sign *s*, and also drop the *n;* as *sermo* (stem, sermon); *leo* (leon), etc.

26. When *quantus* agrees with a noun, it signifies *how great;* but when it is in the neuter gender, and governs a Gen., *how much;* as *quanta* exempla, *how great, important illustrations;* quantum *exemplorum, how many illustrations.*

27. The full form of *sum* is *esum,* the *e* appearing in three forms of the Indic. Pres., and throughout the Impf. Indic. and Subj., etc.

28. Where there are two groups of words forming an antithesis, the order of the first group is changed in the second; thus two of the antithetic words are as far apart as possible, and two as near together as possible; this arrangement making the antithesis more pointed; as CONCORDIA *maxuma, minuma* AVARITIA erat. (See Note 53 to Questions on Cicero.)

29. The order of the conjunctions here named, in point of force, is *at, sed, autem.*

30. A strengthening *n* is inserted in the Pres. of many verbs, as *si-n-o, li-n-o, tem-n-o,* etc., which is retained only in the first root.

31. In several words *p* is inserted between *ms* and *mt* as a support to the voice, giving an easier pronunciation. The organs seem to require such a letter, even if it is not written; as sumo, sum-*p*-si, sum-*p*-tum.

32. The regular form of the comparative of *magnus,* after dropping the strengthening *n,* would be *magior;* dropping the *g* it is *maior,* as it is sometimes written; *i* and *j* were originally the same letter, but the vowel relation was subsequently denoted by *i*, and the consonant relation by *j*, as in *major.*

33. *R* and *s* are often interchangeable letters, the former being often changed into the latter, and the reverse; as from scele*r* comes scele*s*tus, from fe*r*iae, fe*s*tus. So the Part. que*s*tus for que*r*tus, ge*s*tum for ge*r*tum, etc.

34. The stem of *vox* is *voc,* the Nom. sign *s* being appended to the stem, the *c* and *s* combine, and form *x.*

NOTES TO QUESTIONS ON NEPOS.

1. The Greeks did not have, like the Romans, any name to designate the *family* and the *gens*, and hence no surname, as with us; the Greek names are the names of individuals merely, and they never become surnames, as is often the case with us. The Greek generally has but one name, while the Roman has two or more.

2. *Miltiades* here has strictly no grammatical construction. It stands independent, like inscriptions, titles of books, subjects of composition, etc.

3. When the vowel after *qu* is omitted, *q* is changed into *c*. Hence *qu(u)m, cum; loqu(o)r, locutus; qu(o)tidie, cotidie.*

4. The general statement or fact would be the same if *et* were omitted. The use of it gives force, particularity, individuality to *antiquitate*, etc. There is a difference between saying A and B, and both A and B, or, not only A but B. So here.

5. The *et* after *quum* is *correlative* with *et* before *gloria*.

6. Good Latin usage would allow the three *et*'s to be omitted here; so that we could have *antiquitate, gloria, modestia;* but the first two could not be omitted, and the third retained. Hence, all used or all omitted.

7. No uniform or invariable rule for the position of the Gen. can be given; but if the Gen. is prominent or emphatic, — *i. e.*, if the idea expressed by it is more important than that of the noun or adjective by which it is governed, — it stands before the governing word. The position of a Gen. before the governing word does not, however, necessarily make it emphatic, its tendency being to a position before rather than after, independent of emphasis. (See Gram. 279, R.)

8. See Note 32 to Questions on the Fables.

9. The combined force or emphasis of *unus omnium* falls upon *maxime,* — *unus* being frequently joined with the superlative to give it emphasis. Hence *maxime floreret* (was particularly eminent) *unus omnium* (above all others).

10. The regular form of the superlative of *magnus,* from which maxime is derived, would be *magimus;* but an *s* is inserted as an euphonic letter after *g*, and the *g* and *s* combining make *x*.

11. In the first, second, and fourth conjugations the union vowel *e* before *re* of the Inf. combines with the final vowel of the root, and makes the penult vowel of the Inf. long. Thus *amăo* (root *amă*), *amăĕre* = *amāre; docĕo* (root *docĕ*), *docĕĕre* = *docēre; audĭo* (root *audĭ*), *audĭĕre* = *audīre.*

12. The root of *sum* is *es.* The regular form of the Inf., from which the Impf. subjunctive is formed, would then be *esĕre;* but syncopating the *e* after *s*, the *r* is then assimilated to the *s;* hence the Inf. is *esse,* and the Impf. subjunctive is *essem,* etc.

13. "*Jam* always implies a *progression* up to the present time; or from the present to a future time; it thus compares tacitly what is *now* with a former or future state of things. *Nunc* relates to the *present moment; 'now,'* as opposed to *'then.'*" *Johnson's Arnold's Nepos.*

14. The *g* in *cognitum,* and words of the same derivation, does not arise from the *n* of the preposition *con* in composition, but is the initial letter of *nosco,* which has been dropped, — the full form being *gnosco.*

15. Some verbs append *sc* to the root, which is retained only in the parts of the verb formed from the first root. Thus, *no-sc-o, novi, notum.* So *cre-sc-o, pa-sc-o,* etc.

16. The dentals (*d, t*) are sometimes dropped before *s*, and sometimes assimilated to it; hence in the Perf. of *mitto* both the *t*'s are dropped before the ending *si;* thus *mi-si;* but in the supine and Perf. Part. one *t* is assimilated to the *s* of the ending, the other *t* being dropped, as a succession of three consonants would not be admissible;

thus *missus, missum*. In the Perf. of *claudo* the dental *d* is dropped, as *clausi* (for *claudsi*), while in the Perf. of *cedo* it is assimilated, as *cessi* (for *cedsi*). Comp. Note 5 to Questions on the Fables.

17. Words which refer to what precedes generally stand first in the sentence. Hence, demonstrative and relative pronouns, when they relate to a preceding substantive or statement, are always placed first. *Krebs's Guide for Writing Latin.*

18. The *er* and *or* of the stem of neuter nouns is often changed into *us* in forming the Nom., as *gener, genus; corpor, corpus.*

19. See Note 12.

20. Different prepositions in English are used to express the relation of the Latin objective Gen. governed by a noun; as ejus *demigrationis* societatem, *participation* IN *this emigration.* So admonitio *virtutis, encouragement* TO *virtue; praemium industriae, reward* FOR *industry;* peritia *historiae, acquaintance* WITH *history; deorum* opinio, *belief* IN *the gods. Krebs's Guide.*

21. Some verbs of the third conjugation form their second and third roots like verbs of the fourth conjugation, as peto, petĕre, *petivi, petitum.* So *cupio, quaero*, etc.

22. When mutes come together they must be of the same order, smooth with smooth, hard with hard, etc. Hence, when the smooth or soft *g* of *deligo* comes to stand before the hard *t* in the third root, it is changed into the hard mute *c*.

23. The stem of *Apollinem* is Apollin; but some nouns of the third Dec. whose stem ends in *n*, drop that letter, and where the stem vowel is *i*, change the *i* into *o;* hence stem *homin*, Nom. *homo;* stem *Apollin*, Nom. *Apollo* (see Note 25 to Questions on the Fables).

24. See Note 34 to Questions on the Fables.

25. The final *r* of *uterentur* is the sign of the passive, the *u* before it being merely a connecting vowel, connecting the passive sign and *t*, the sign of the third person.

26. Neuter or intransitive verbs can be used only impersonally in the passive; since in the active voice they have no Acc. which can

be converted into the subject of the verb in the passive. Hence, *invidet mihi, he envies me,* but *invidetur mihi, I am envied,* not invideor.

27. The *i* in *capĭo,* and other words in *-io* of the third conjugation, does not belong to the root, but is a strengthening letter. This vowel is dropped in all the endings of the Pres. Indic. Act. and Pass., beginning with a consonant, and is therefore retained only in the first Pers. Sing. and third Pers. Pl.; as *capio, capior, capiunt, capiuntur.* The *i* in *capĭs, capĭmus, capĭtis* is not this strengthening *i,* but is merely the union vowel. If it were the strengthening *i,* it would be long in these forms, as is the case in the fourth conjugation, where the *i* is part of the root, and combines with the union vowel *i,* and becomes long; hence, *audĭo, audīs, audīmus, audītis.* The syllable *it,* however, of the third Pers. Sing. is short, even in the fourth conjugation.

28. See Note 31 to Questions on the Fables.

29. In *oratio recta, fecissent* would be in the Fut. Perf., and *futura* in the simple future; hence, *si id fecerint,* incepta prospera *erunt.*

30. In Note 15 it was said that some verbs append *sc* to the root; this is done when the root ends in a vowel, as *no-sc-o;* but when the root ends in a consonant, *isc* is appended instead of *sc,* otherwise three consonants would come together; as *profis-isc-or, reviv-isc-o, concup-isc-o.*

31. *Sua sponte* is the predominant usage, *sponte sua* seldom, in the best period of the language, except in the poets.

32. When compounded with a verb, *in* very rarely has a negative sense. In *ignosco, ignoro,* it has a negative force.

33. *Facturos* in *oratio recta* would be in the simple future: *we will do it* (*faciemus*).

34. Before the dentals *d* and *t, m* is changed into the dental *n;* hence, *eundem* for *eumdem, tantus* for *tamtus.* In this way letters of the same order are brought together, and are more easily pronounced.

NOTES TO QUESTIONS ON CICERO.

1. See Note 34 to Questions on Nepos.

2. The *dem* in *tandem* is a demonstrative suffix, the same as in *idem*.

3. In imperative and interrogative sentences *tandem* has the meaning of *I pray, I ask,* thereby giving emphasis to the expression with which it is connected.

4. The form in *-re,* instead of *-ris,* is not usual in the second Pers. Sing. Indic. Pass., as the form in *-re* would be the same as that of the Pres. Inf. Acc., and might be easily mistaken for it; *e. g., amare* for *amaris, docēre* for *doceris.* But in the subjunctive Pres. Pass. the form in *-re* may be used, as it is not liable to be mistaken for any other form; *amēre* for *ameris; carpare* for *carparis.*

5. *Furor* is an appropriate word to denote the recklessness of a seditious person.

6. The metaphor implied in *eludet* is derived from combatants or gladiators, who by a skilful motion of the body avoid the thrusts of their antagonists.

7. *Iste* is compounded of *is* and the pronominal suffix *te,*—the same suffix that is appended to *tu* to strengthen it, as *tute.*

8. Two pronouns in a sentence, referring to each other, are usually placed near together. *Krebs's Guide.*

9. The bad sense of *iste* arises from its frequent use in addressing the defendant or opponent in courts of justice.

10. See Note 21 to Questions on the Fables.

11. In Cicero, *quem ad finem* does not mean *to what end,* but *how long.*

12. In the earlier language, the Acc. Sing. of pronouns was strengthened by reduplicating the form; as *meme, tete, sese.* The reduplicated *sese* is found both in the Sing. and Pl. in the best period of the language.

13. The question introduced by *ne* does not determine whether the answer is to be *yes* or *no.* The question with *ne* is asked for information, whether the thing is or is not so.

14. By separating the governing and governed words from each other, the mind of the hearer or reader is kept in suspense till it reaches the governing or the governed word; in this way a stronger impression is made.

15. In times of danger a guard or garrison was placed upon the Palatine hill, as it was situated in the central part of the city, and whoever had possession of it could defend the city.

16. Cities were not in a circular form; but from their compactness, and from their being surrounded by a wall, the word denoting a city is properly derived from *orbis, a circle.*

17. Watches were posted through the whole city by the decree of the Senate. See *Sallust's Catiline*, c. 30.

18. During the Republic there was no standing police force. Sentinels, however, were employed on occasions of danger.

19. The temple of Jupiter Stator stood near the foot of the Palatine hill.

20. The temple of Jupiter Stator.

21. Some editions have two or three instances of a Perf. in *-ēre* for *-erunt;* it is probable, however, that Cicero never used the perfect form in *-ēre,* but that this was the work of some copyist. Neither Caesar nor Nepos uses it.

22. See Note 11 to Questions on Nepos.

23. A question with *non* expresses surprise that the thing is not so (does not take place), and a doubt of the possibility of its being denied (*Madvig's Lat. Gram.*). Hence, in the passage here, *Is it possible that you do not see*, etc.?

24. See Note 27 to Questions on Nepos.

25. See Note 22 to Questions on Nepos.

26. Besides the idea of a *past act*, the Perf. definite often denotes the *present state*, or *continuance of the result;* hence *constrictam, having been bound*, and the state continuing, *being now bound.*

27. The conspiracy is here compared to a wild beast that is chained.

28. *Nonne* would imply an affirmative answer, it being assumed that the person addressed knows and admits the thing to be so. For the meaning of a question with *non*, see Note 23.

29. The union vowel *i* in the termination *is* combines with the short *e* of *video*, and lengthens it. Comp. Note 27 to the Questions on Nepos.

30. For *propior* and *proximus*, an old positive, *propus*, must be assumed. The superlative of such a positive would be *propsimus;* the *ps* forming *x*, the word becomes *proximus.*

31. *Summus* comes from *supremus* by syncopating *re*, and assimilating the *p* to the *m* after it.

32. The change of *a* to *e*, as well as the quantity of *e*, is explained by the reduplication of Greek verbs beginning with a short vowel, as ἦχα from ἄγω.

33. The Gen. Sing. of nouns in *-ius* and *-ium* was probably in *-i*, instead of *ii*, till the time of Augustus, though there is some discrepancy in the MSS. on this subject.

34. The stem of *mos* is *mor;* but *s* and *r* being interchangeable letters, the termination in *s* was preferred. Compare *honor* and *honos*, *arbor* and *arbos*, the poets preferring the forms in *s*.

35. The omission of the connective gives animation and force to the discourse, — the mind being directed only to what is important to the thought.

36. The second *v* in *vivo* combines with the tense sign *s* in the second root, and forms *x* (*vixi*), and in the third root is changed into *c* before *t* (*victum*).

37. The force of *immo* is strengthened or made emphatic by *vero*.

38. By *publici consilii* is meant the deliberation in regard to the interests and safety of the state; and the force of the expression consists in the fact that the state is in so deplorable a condition that the man who is plotting for her destruction takes part in this deliberation.

39. See Note 29 to Questions on the Fables.

40. Neither the Perf. nor Plupf. Indic. of *oportet* would imply that the act was performed at the time when it should have been, but both of them would imply that the time for doing the act was past; while the Impf. Indic. implies that the time for doing the act is not past; the act ought to have been done long ago, but it was not done; it ought to be done still, and may be done.

41. For the sake of euphony, in poetry, also for the sake of the quantity, a consonant, particularly a liquid, is sometimes doubled. In some instances the doubled letter would be pronounced if it were not written. Hence *ferri*, Pas. Inf. of *fero; os, oss-is; mel, mell-is; far, farr-is; mille* and *mīle; littera* and *lītera*.

42. *Omnis*, as the Greek *πᾶς*, usually stands after the pronouns to which it belongs.

43. *Jamdiu*, implying past time, necessarily requires the verb to which it belongs to be translated by a past tense: *You have been for a long time plotting, and are still.*

44. Scipio, a private man, is contrasted with Cicero the consul; Gracchus with Catiline; a slight attempt against the state with its destruction; the Roman republic with the whole world.

45. A very short word usually precedes a longer one.

46. Certain expressions have a uniform arrangement of the words, as *pontifex maximus, patres conscripti, populus Romanus*. So in English, *safe and sound, fire and water, hope and fear*. The fixed phrases in English, however, are often different from the Latin, as *by sea and land* (*terra marique*), *by fire and sword* (*ferro ignique*), etc.

47. See Note 14 above.

48. Cicero here speaks for rhetorical effect, and does not give a true view of the efforts of Gracchus for a revolution. He elsewhere speaks in a very different tone of Gracchus.

49. *Nam* is often a transition particle, being used when the speaker passes on to a remark *occasioned* by the former sentence, but not containing any cause or reason. *Arnold's Latin Prose.*

50. The *d* which appears in *illud, id,* and the like, is probably the same as the demonstrative δε in Greek, as *τόδε, this here.* It therefore increases the demonstrative force of the word.

51. *Quod* with the Indic. here, as in other similar passages, is nearly equivalent to the Acc. with the Inf. Indeed, the Acc. with the Inf. (*C. Servilium Ahalam ..... occidisse*) might have been substituted for it with slight difference of meaning. *Quod,* however, is more appropriate when the verb following it is in a past tense. Comp. *Zumpt's Lat. Gram.,* 626, Note 1.

52. In composition there is a frequent change of vowels, as *a* into *e* before two consonants, and into *i* before one: *inermis* (*in* and *arma*), *expers* (*ex* and *pars*), *inimicus* (*in* and *amicus*); so *coerceo* (*con* and *arceo*). Comp. Note 37 to Questions on Virgil.

53. The figure by which the order of the words in two or more groups is changed, is called *Chiasmus* (a placing crosswise). See further, Note 28 to Questions on the Fables. Comp. also Catil., third Orat. 6, quod URBEM *incendiis, caede* CIVES ..... *liberassem.*

54. The *senatus consultum* here referred to was passed on the 21st of October, 63 B. C.

55. The formula by which the consuls were invested with supreme power was: Darent operam consules ne quid respublica detrimenti caperet. See Chap. 2 of this oration.

NOTES TO QUESTIONS ON VIRGIL.

1. The tomb of Virgil is shown at Naples. Niebuhr, incredulous as he was in regard to all matters of mere tradition, believed this to be the tomb of Virgil.

2. In the Aeneid, Aeneas is a purely mythical character. Under this name Virgil has undoubtedly described the character and achievements of some other person, perhaps those of Augustus.

3. The first seven lines, which may be termed the proem, contain the subject of the poem.

4. When Virgil says that he *sings* of arms and the man, etc., he means particularly that he is to describe these in poetry. Sometimes, however, the recitation of poetry was accompanied by music.

5. See Note 23 to Questions on the Fables.

6. The word *Dactyl* is derived from the Greek *δάκτυλος*, *a finger*, because a dactyl has one long syllable and two short ones, just as the finger has one long part or joint and two short ones. The word *Spondee* is derived from *σπονδή*, *libation, treaty*; because in the services connected with these, slow, solemn, *spondaic* melodies were used.

7. The greatest number of syllables in a hexameter line is seventeen; all the feet may be dactyls except the last. The least number is thirteen; all may be spondees except the fifth.

8. Authority or the use of the poets really determines the quantity of all syllables; and the rules themselves even are based on this usage. The rules, therefore, only group together certain forms or endings, etc., whose vowels have a uniform quantity, either long or short; *i. e.*, the rules are only the exponents of the quantity as determined by the use of the poets. But if the quantity of every vowel of every word was determined by rule, the rules would be so numerous

as to be of little value. Therefore, when it is said that a particular syllable is long or short by authority, it is only meant that it does not come under any of the *general* rules.

9. A short syllable is often made long in the Arsis, by the stress of voice which falls upon it.

10. See Note 4 to Questions on Nepos.

11. *Vis* has been found to be used in all its cases, though the Gen. and Dat. Sing. are very rare.

12. See Note 31 to Questions on Cicero.

13. See Note 25 to Questions on the Fables.

14. *Etiam* would be commonly used in good prose, instead of *et* here.

15. *Dum*, signifying *while*, may be followed by the subjunctive when a *design, purpose*, or *wish* is expressed.

16. The stem of the second root of *fero* is *tol;* the third root then would regularly be *tolatum*, and dropping the *o*, *tlatum*. The *t* of the last form being dropped on account of the uneuphonic combination of *tl*, the third root becomes *latum*. For the change of *o* into *u* in *tuli*, see Note 27.

17. The name of the country was in most cases derived from the name of the people, and not the reverse. *Latium* was then the country of the *Latini*.

18. In *mihi*, only *mi* is root, and *hi* is the Dat. ending. *Mihi*, particularly in poetry, was often contracted into *mi*.

19. In Cicero's time, and before, *causa* was written with two *s*'s. All languages have a varying orthography; the variance being greatest at periods remote from each other, but also to some extent manifest at any given period. There was often a difference between the orthography in manuscripts, on coins, and inscriptions on stone. Hence, *numus* and *nummus; annulus* and *anulus; poena* and *paena; vult* and *volt; coelum* and *caelum; genetrix* and *genitrix; toties* and *totiens; conjux* and *conjunx; litera* and *littera; haud* and *haut*, etc.

20. *Quid* in itself has no signification kindred or related to *dolens;* the actual cognate word is to be considered as understood, and *quid* is regarded as the attributive of such cognate word, and of course stands in the same case as that word would if supplied. In this way *quid* can be said to be a cognate accusative.

21. *V* before a consonant, particularly *t*, changes into *u;* as *volutum* (from *volvo*), *solutum* (from *solvo*), *fautum* (from *faveo*), — *v* having originally both a vowel and consonant *force*, and the consonant force being uneuphonic before another consonant, assumes, for the sake of euphony, in cases like those here given, its vowel relation in the form of *u*. On the contrary, the vowel *u* sometimes takes a consonant force, and changes into *v;* as ga*u*deo, ga*v*isus.

22. *E* is changed into *u*, especially before a single *l*, or usually before *l* followed by a consonant; as *pello, pepuli, pulsum; vello, vulsum.*

23. Besides the other grounds for the use of the plural of nouns, the poets not unfrequently use it either for emphasis or for the metre.

24. In poetry, words that require to be made emphatic receive a special emphasis by being placed at the beginning or end of the line.

25. The name *Mare Mediterraneum* first occurs about A.D. 250, the Roman name previous being *Mare Internum.*

26. *Unus*, as an intensive word, occurs much more frequently with the superlative than with the comparative.

27. *O* frequently interchanges with *u;* as *corpus* for *corpor*, *vult* for *volt*, *humanus* from *homo.*

28. The Greek has a past active participle, and would take *Samo* in the Acc. after it; but the Latin, having no past active participle, can express the relation only by the passive participle in the Abl. absolute.

29. The prevailing Hiatus in Virgil is in the Arsis, more seldom in the Thesis. In line 16 the effect of the Hiatus is prevented by the Caesura, and by the division in the line.

30. The old ablative from which *hic* comes was *h(o)ic* or *h(e)ic* = *hic.*

31. In Virgil the penult *i* of *illius* is oftener short than long.

32. As *hoc* here refers to *Carthago,* which is feminine, but takes the gender of *regnum,* there is strictly an attraction of gender.

33. See Note 12 to Questions on Nepos.

34. See Note 4 to Questions on Nepos.

35. See Note 50 to Questions on Cicero.

36. *Qui* usually stands the first word in its clause in prose.

37. *A* in composition is usually changed into the lighter vowel *i* before a single consonant, but before two consonants into *e;* as *inimicus* (in + amicus), *abigo* (ab + ago), *conjicio* (con + jacio), *abripio* (ab + rapio), *coerceo* (con + arceo), *abreptus* (ab + raptus).

38. *Spretae* is formed from the theme *spreo.*

39. See Note 22 to Questions on Nepos.

NOTES TO QUESTIONS ON THE ANABASIS.

1. Socrates had no particular place where he gave his instructions; sometimes he taught in the groves of the Academy, sometimes in the Lyceum, or on the banks of the Ilissus, or in the streets of Athens.

2. Proxenus had come to Athens to attend the instructions of Gorgias the rhetorician, and while there had formed an acquaintance with Xenophon.

3. Scillus was given to Xenophon by the Lacedemonians, they having taken it from the Eleans.

4. The expedition left Ephesus about the 7th of February, and Sardis about the 6th of March.

5. Cyrus was not quite seventeen when he was appointed satrap.

6. Cyrus's satrapy included Lydia, Phrygia, and Cappadocia, being between that of Pharnabazus on the north, and that of Tissaphernes on the south.

7. Cyrus was invested with higher powers than the other two satraps, and stood to them nearly in the relation of governor-general.

8. The cause for the disappearance of δ in the Nom. does not exist in the Gen., for in the Gen. it stands before a vowel, but in the Nom. before σ, which is an uneuphonic combination. Hence σ rejects δ in the Nom.

9. The σ appended to the stem of nouns of the third Dec. is the sign of the Nom., sometimes called the gender-sign, as it is appended to masculine and feminine nouns. Comp. Note 17 to Questions on the Fables.

10. The syllable of reduplication γι rejects ε of the stem (γεν) in γίγνομαι.

11. The ε rejected by the improper reduplication γι, reappears in all the tenses where γι is dropped.

12. The combination of a liquid and σ was not euphonious; hence the σ was either dropped after a liquid (as in στελῶ for στέλσω), or a vowel was assumed to obviate the harshness. Hence, for the formation of the Fut. of γίγνομαι, an ε is assumed with the stem γεν, which then becomes γενε, and this ε in forming the Fut. is lengthened into η, as in contract verbs.

13. The numeral δύω is scarcely used at all in Attic; δύο, both in Attic and Ionic.

14. The particles μέν ..... δέ stand in contrasted clauses, though the contrast is often a slight one.

15. The stem of εἰμί is ἐς; the σ being dropped, as a compensation ε is lengthened into ει.

16. The clause commencing with ἐπεί is an adverbial clause; as it denotes the time when the action expressed by ἐβούλετο took place. The same clause, however, under other circumstances might be a substantive clause; as in the expression, "I knew when Darius was sick," — the clause "when Darius was sick" being the object of the verb *knew*.

17. The inferential particle οὖν is much stronger than ἄρα, — the latter implying only a slight consequence.

18. The original or assumed form of the article was τός, — the Nom. sign σ being dropped in the Nom. Sing. masculine, and the τ in the Nom. Sing. and Pl. masculine and feminine.

19. The Greek avoided the stiffer form of the Plupf., and substituted for it the more pliant Aor., except where special precision in the relation of time was required. For this reason the Aor. is often found where the Plupf. might have been expected.

20. In the combination καὶ δέ the word on which the force of καί falls, stands between these particles. Hence in the passage referred to: "and appointed him *general also*."

21. The η before γ in στρατηγόν would regularly be long α (στρατᾱγόν), as in λοχᾱγός; but as a second α in the word would be uneuphonic, the α is changed into η.

22. The σ in πᾶς is the sign of the Nom. Comp. Note 9; also Note 17 to Questions on the Fables.

23. Αὐτῶν is a more quiet, or less emphatic, form than τούτων would be.

24. The regular form instead of ἵστημι would be σίστημι, — σι being the reduplication (Comp. Lat. *sisto*). For the sake of a more euphonic form, the sibilant σ is exchanged for the aspirate, which transferred to ι makes it ἱ. So the regular Perf. Act. would be σέστηκα, but by a similar change it becomes ἕστηκα.

25. The old pronominal use of the article is infrequent in Attic Greek; this use of it occurs, however, in all periods of the language, particularly in such forms as ὁ μέν, ὁ δέ; οἱ μέν, οἱ δέ; τὸν μέν, τὸν δέ, etc.

26. The regular form of the Perf. would be λέληφα; but the λ is dropped as not euphonious, and, as a compensation, ε is lengthened into ει.

27. Ὡς with the participle denotes the view, opinion, or purpose of the agent or actor; here not the view or purpose of Xenophon, but that of Artaxerxes.

28. Some words are defective in certain tenses; and such defective tenses are supplied by the corresponding tenses of other words of a similar meaning.

29. The Greek α may be either long or short; in the word κινδυνεύσας, the α was long by position before the dropping of ντ; but after the dropping of these letters, it becomes naturally long, being lengthened as a compensation for the omitted letters. But ε is not both long and short in itself; therefore, when ντ of ἀτιμασθείς is dropped, ε is lengthened into ει. The α, then, is lengthened in its nature, and ε in its form.

30. The ὁ in ὅπως is the relative ὁ, the stem of ὅς, — σ being the Nom. sign. The ὁ in ὁποῖος, ὁπόσος, ὁπότε, etc., has the same origin.

31. The ι *subscript* was originally written in the line, and pronounced. Subsequently, when it came to be omitted in the pronunciation, it was dropped in the writing, but was afterwards restored, so as to preserve the original form of the words to which it belonged, being then written under (subscript) the word, instead of in the line, as originally.

32. The repetitions of the action in the principal clause must balance or be equal to those in the introductory clause; such repeated actions in the principal clause are appropriately expressed only by the Impf. Indic.

33. The expression τῶν παρὰ βασιλέως, with its connected clause, is literally translated: "Now whoever *of the* [*those*] *from the king* came to him" (from time to time).

34. Besides its genitive relation here, βασιλέως has also the relation of a Dat. with παρά. Thus the whole expression would be: Ὅστις δ' ἀφικνοῖτο τῶν [ὄντων παρὰ βασιλεῖ] παρὰ βασιλέως, etc. (whoever of those being with the king came from the king). This construction is not infrequent.

35. The particle τέ was, in the earlier periods of the language, joined with certain classes of words to give them a connective force. But as the language improved, these words came to have a connective force of themselves. The τέ was then no longer needed, and was wholly superfluous with such words; it was therefore generally omitted in Attic Greek. Some few words, however, retained it, even in the best periods of the language; as ὥστε, οἷός τε, etc.

36. The position of παρ' ἑαυτῷ in the phrase τῶν παρ' ἑαυτῷ βαρβάρων, between the article and its noun, gives it an adjective or attributive relation. The phrase, literally translated, is: "the with-himself barbarians."

37. The verb ἔχειν with an adverb is generally equivalent to εἰμί

with the same adverb; as ἔχειν εὐνοϊκῶς, *to have themselves well disposed, to be well disposed;* ἔχειν οὕτως, *to have itself so, to be so.*

38. The particle ὡς is often joined with superlatives to strengthen them or increase their force. The force of ὡς, therefore, falls upon the superlative.

39. Where ὡς is used to strengthen the superlative, as stated in Note 38, some part of δύναμαι, or an equivalent expression, is expressed or understood; very often understood. Ὡς, therefore, in such cases, is a simple connective, — connecting the word which the superlative strengthens with some part of δύναμαι expressed or understood. In the passage here referred to, ὡς connects ἐδύνατο with ἐπικρυπτόμενος, *concealing himself especially as he was able, as much as he in any way could;* hence *as secretly as possible.*

40. The particle ὅτι is strictly a pronoun, and virtually retains its pronominal force where it is used to strengthen a comparative or superlative. Its real force in this and similar clauses can be seen by analyzing the one in which it here stands. Supplying the ellipsis, the sentence would stand thus: ὅπως λάβοι βασιλέα οὕτως ἀπαρασκεύαστον, ὡς ὅ,τι ἀπαρασκευότατόν ἐστι, *that he might take the king so unprepared, as whatever is most unprepared,* i. e., *as unprepared as* POSSIBLE. See *White's Anabasis.*

41. Ποιεῖσθαι συλλογήν means *to make a levy* for one's self, like the Latin *comparare sibi;* while ποιεῖν συλλογήν is simply *to make a levy,* — it not being determined by the expression itself for whom it is made.

42. In the sentence commencing ὁπόσας, φυλακάς is attracted into the relative clause, and into the case of the relative (ὁπόσας). Putting φυλακάς in its own clause and case, the sentence would stand: φυλακῶν, ὁπόσας εἶχε, etc., — φυλακῶν being then governed by φρουράρχοις.

43. A medial mute is inserted between μρ and νρ to soften the pronunciation; as μεσημ-β-ρία, ἄμ-β-ροτος, ἄν-δ-ρες.

44. The Latin inserts *p* between *mt* and *ms*, etc., as a support for the voice, it being difficult for the organs to avoid pronouncing the *p*,

even if it is not written; as *emo, em-p-si, em-p-tum, tem-p-tare, tem-p-lum* (from τέμνω). Comp. Note 31 to Questions on the Fables.

45. On the same principle as in Greek and Latin, a mute is inserted in English between *m* and the consonant following it, the latter more commonly being *l* or *t*; as *hum-b-le* (for *humle*), *mum-b-le, tum-b-le, tem-p-t, exem-p-t, tem-p-le.*

46. Ὡς with the participle may be rendered: *saying that, pretending that, alleging that, on the ground that, because, as though, as if,* and the like.

47. Ἐπιβουλεύοντος without ὡς would denote merely the *fact* that Tissaphernes was plotting; with ὡς, it is the reason, as given by Cyrus (which reason may not actually exist), for issuing orders to raise forces.

48. In the phrase καὶ γάρ, the καί suggested to the eye or ear of the Greek the connection of the clause in which it stood with that which preceded; but in English the connection is not expressed with the same fulness or precision; therefore this καί is rarely translated. In the Greek it is generally equivalent to what might be expressed in English by: *and this was so, for* (γάρ).

49. See Note 24.

50. Ἕστηκα, the simple Perf. of ἀφεστήκεσαν, signifies *I have placed myself;* and as the Perf. denotes the continuance of the *result,* the word denotes a *present state,* hence, *I stand;* the Impf. would then denote the *continuance of the state;—had revolted, and were then in a state of revolt.*

51. Οὗτος is compounded of the article ὁ and αὐτός. Where the article ends in an ο sound, as ου, ω, etc.. οὗτος has ου in the penult; otherwise αυ.

52. Βουλευομένους is here the complement of προαισθόμενος; the action or time denoted by the complementary participle is usually *prior* to that of the word of which it is the complement; the act of *plotting* (βουλευομένους) must have been prior to the perception of it (προαισθόμενος).

53. In English the word *namely* is often used to introduce a word or clause explanatory of what precedes. The Latin and Greek very often use no corresponding word here.

54. See Note 25.

55. Where a pronoun refers to a preceding statement, and hence would be regularly in the neuter gender, but is conformed to that of a following noun, there is said to be an *attraction of gender*. Comp. Note 32 to Questions on Virgil.

56. The position of *αὕτη* between *καί* and *αὖ* is emphatic. Compare above the position of *στρατηγόν* between *καί* and *δέ*, and Note 20.

57. In the formation of the Pres. *πράττω*, a strengthening *τ* is added to the stem *πραγ*, and this *τ* assimilates the *γ* to itself; hence the two *τ*'s.

58. The position of *πρὸς ἑαυτόν* between *τῆς* and *ἐπιβουλῆς* makes it an attributive of *ἐπιβουλῆς*. Preserving the force of the original, then, the English would be: "the against-himself plot."

59. The relation of *manner* or *means* denoted by the Part. *πολεμοῦντα*, would be naturally expressed in Latin by the gerund in the Abl. The Greek supplies the place of the Latin gerund partly by the Part. and partly by the Inf. with the Article in the Dat.

60. The relative is attracted into the case of the antecedent, generally, only with such verbs as govern an Acc.

61. Generally only the verbals in *-τός* and *-τέος* and the Perf. Pass. take the Dat. of the agent.

62. *Χερσόνησος* was the older and original form. The later Attics, after Thucydides, adopted the form *Χεῤῥόνησος*, changing the *ρσ* into *ῤῥ*.

63. If *τῇ καταντιπέρας Ἀβύδου* were placed between *ἐν* and *Χεῤῥονήσῳ*, the meaning would be the same as with the present position. Literally rendered, then, it would be: "the over-against-Abydus Chersonese."

64. The respective relations of *αὐτῷ* and *εἰς τὴν τροφήν* can be

expressed by a literal translation as follows: "so that they even contributed money *for him for the support* of his soldiers."

65. The accentuation of οἴκοι (at home) may be explained in two ways: 1, as a Dat. for οἴκῳ; the ultimate being long, the word could not be a properispomenon. This is the usual explanation. 2. The word may be a syncopated form for οἴκοφι, the φι being an old Dat. ending. The accent is then proparoxytone and regular.

66. The word ξένους is strictly governed by εἰς here; but the whole expression εἰς δισχιλίους ξένους is a second Acc. governed by αἰτεῖ, just as a preposition and its case often stands as the subject Nom. of the verb.

67. Οὕτω is equivalent to a protasis of the proposition, and might be translated: "if he should receive them."

68. The particle ἄν standing with περιγενόμενος shows that the participle is subject to a condition, the condition being contained in οὕτω. The force of the whole expression, then, could be given thus: "saying (ὡς), if he should receive them (οὕτω), he would be superior to his opponents."

69. In Attic prose κελεύειν takes the Acc. with the Inf. Πρόξενον is then the subject Acc. of παραγενέσθαι.

70. It is not certainly known when the written accents were first introduced, but probably about two hundred years before Christ. They were evidently introduced for the purpose of preserving the pronunciation of the language in its purity, at a time when it was in danger of being corrupted.

71. The personal pronouns μοῦ, σοῦ, ἡμῶν, αὐτοῦ, etc., stand before or after the noun by which they are governed; but the demonstrative τούτου, and the reflexives ἑαυτοῦ, σεαυτοῦ stand between the article and the noun, or after the noun with the article repeated. Hence, instead of τῇ ἑαυτοῦ χώρᾳ, it could have been written τῇ χώρᾳ τῇ ἑαυτοῦ.

72. The rules which determine the place of the accent are obtained like the rules of Prosody, by bringing under a general principle

classes of words having a uniform accent. Thus, neuter nouns of the third Dec. generally take the accent as far back as the nature of the final syllable will permit; as *στράτευμα, χρήματα, πράγματα*; so nouns in *-ις* Gen. *-εως*, follow the same rule; likewise, those of the first Dec. in *α* preceded by a mute (except those derived from verbs), as *θάλατταν*; abstract nouns in *-ειᾱ* from verbs in *-εύω* are paroxytones, as *βασιλείαν*; while concretes in *-ειᾰ*, or those derived from adjectives in *-ης* are proparoxytones. Those in *-ευς* are oxytones, as *βασιλεύς*; so those in *-ας*, Gen. *-αδος*, as *φυγάς*; likewise those in *η*, derived from the Perf. Pass., second Perf., or second Aor. Act., as *συλλογήν, ἐπιβουλῆς, τροφήν*, while most others in *η* preceded by a a mute are paroxytones.

These are but illustrations of the general rules (subject to exceptions) relating to the place of the accent. The words here given as examples are from the first chapter of the Anabasis.

73. The *τ* in *Μίλητος* is changed into *σ* in *Μιλησίων* by the influence of the *ι*. So frequently, as *πλούσιος* from *πλοῦτος*; *οὐσία* from *ὀντία*.

74. Similar words are placed near each other.

NOTES TO QUESTIONS ON HOMER.

1. The Iliad was known in European Greece some more than 500 years B. C., but in Ionia or Asiatic Greece much earlier.

2. Originally the Iliad was not divided into books, as at present; the different parts were then designated merely by the subjects treated; hence, *Λοιμός*, Μῆνις. If there was occasion to refer to or quote this part of the Iliad, it would be quoted by the subject; as Homer *ἐν τῷ Λοιμῷ* remarks, *i. e.*, in the part of the Iliad where he describes the Plague. Comp. a similar mode of quotation in the Scriptures: "How in the bush God spake unto him;" *i. e.*, how in the passage where the burning bush is described.

3. Poetic compositions were sometimes recited in a chanting style; sometimes they were sung, with a lute or guitar (cithara) as an accompaniment. The word *ᾄδειν*, however, often signifies merely to describe in verse. Comp Note 4 to Questions on Virgil.

4. O may be lengthened into *ου* before liquids and *σ*; as *Οὐλύμποιο*, line 44, and *οὐρῆας*, line 50.

5. The termination *-εα* is very rarely contracted in Homer; hence *ἀμφηρεφέα*, line 45, *ἀεικέα*, line 97, *ἄλγεα*, line 110.

6. The elision of the final *α* in *ἄλγεα* and retaining the augment of *ἔθηκεν* occasion the feminine caesura in the fifth foot, which was a favorite one with Homer. If the line is read without the elision, and with the omission of the augment, the difference will be readily perceived.

7. The *ν* in *ἔθηκεν* is usually considered the paragogic *ν*; but it is regarded also, by Stadelmann and some other eminent scholars, as a strengthening *ν* at the end of the verse, belonging to the original and full form. Hermann thinks it is added at the end of a verse to a

short syllable, that the voice may rest on that syllable, before it proceeds to the next verse.

8. Where two different forms of an oblique case are referred to the same Nom., but for one of which a different Nom. must be assumed, there is the so-called figure of *Metaplasm.* Thus the genitives Ἀΐδαο and Ἄϊδος are referred to the same Nom. Ἀΐδης; but for the form Ἄϊδος a form Ἄϊς must be assumed.

9. The feminine caesura in the fourth foot was avoided by Homer as undesirable.

10. The particle τέ, here and usually, stands after the word it connects with a preceding word.

11. The full expression, instead of ἐξ οὗ, would be ἐκ χρόνου ἐξ οὗ.

12. The particle δή is often joined with words denoting time, to give them explicitness, or to add force to the temporal idea which they contain.

13. The τέ after τίς is apparently pleonastic. Generally the English would not use any corresponding word. By the use of it Homer keeps up the connection in *form* between this sentence and the preceding one. Comp. Note 35 to Questions on the Anabasis.

14. When the accent of an enclitic unites with a preceding oxytone, the two words become one in respect to accentuation. Hence the accent stands just as if the two words were written together, as ἄρσφωε. But the accent of a word is never depressed on the penult or antepenult, as λόγος, τεκμήριον. Not, then, ἀρσφωε, but ἄρσφωε.

15. Τόν here, and generally in Homer, has a strictly pronominal force, — being the object of the verb, and Χρύσην in apposition with it; thus, "because he dishonored *him* — Chryses the priest." Comp. in Book I., lines 348 and 488, where the noun in apposition is separated from the pronoun, viz., γυνή from ἡ, and υἱός from ὁ.

16. It is probable that originally dual forms were only modifications of the plural forms; but in process of time usage appropriated

the dual forms to express only dual relations. In the earlier period of the language, therefore, the dual and plural would be used interchangeably, and the numeral δύω would not unnaturally be joined with the dual.

17. The grammatical structure of a language is comparatively loose in its earlier periods, and becomes grammatically more exact as it improves. Hence Homer allows a looseness of construction which Xenophon would not. In the strictest sense, the Inf. λῦσαι is not here used as an imperative, but depends on some word of *willing* understood, as ἔθελε, βούλου, etc. But as the mind so readily supplies such an imperative, we accustom ourselves, in loose language, to say that the Inf. is used as an Imperative.

18. The Greek was originally written in capitals, without spaces between the words, as follows:

ΕΝΘΑΛΛΟΙΜΕΝΠΑΝΤΕΣΕΠΕΥΦΗΜΗΣΑΝΑΧΑΙΟΙ.[1]

19. Cursive writing, *i. e.*, like our common Greek texts, is first found in manuscripts in the eighth century of our era. The cursive letters, however, were used to some extent long before.

20. Hiatus was particularly unpleasant to the Greek ear. Various means were therefore used to avoid it, as elision, contraction, crasis, paragogic ν. Hence it occurs much more frequently in Latin than in Greek, as may be readily seen by a comparison.

21. Some nouns of the third Dec. reject the gender-sign σ, and as a compensation lengthen the short final vowel of the stem. Hence γέρων instead of γέρονς.

22. The Ionic dialect continued to be spoken and written till about three hundred years before Christ. About two hundred and fifty years before Christ, the Attic had superseded it. See *Sophocles's Glossary of Later and Byzantine Greek*, p. 2.

23. The pronoun μιν stands here in the Acc., governed by ἔπεισιν, Homer loosely placing after a verb of motion the Acc. of a person or thing on which the action of the verb terminates. In Attic Greek

1 Line 22 of the First Book of the Iliad.

such accusatives would be governed by a preposition. The Acc. ἱστόν (line 31) comes under the same principle.

24. The open or uncontracted form of verbs in -άω occurs in Homer only in single words and forms. The open form always occurs with ὑλάω, and such as have a long α for their characteristic, or whose stem is a monosyllable; as διψάων, πεινάων, ἔχραε (from χράω). See *Kühner's Elementary Greek Gram.*

25. Instead of the open forms of verbs in -άω referred to in Note 24, the vowel produced by contraction is resolved where the verse requires it. One of the principles on which the resolution takes place is as follows: When the syllable preceding the syllables to be contracted is short, and the second of the syllables to be contracted is long, ο is inserted before ω or ῳ; as ὁράω, ὁρῶ, ὁρόω; ὁραοῦσι, ὁρῶσι, ὁρόωσι; ἀντιάωσαν, ἀντιῶσαν, ἀντιόωσαν. In like manner short α is inserted before α or ᾳ.

26. In forming the Attic νέῃ from the Epic νέηαι, the η absorbs the α and the ι is subscribed.

27. In Latin the vowels are to the consonants as four to five.[1]

28. In Greek the proportion of the vowels to the consonants is greater than in the Latin, being as six to seven.

29. The diphthongs in Latin are to those in Greek about as one to six.

1 On this and the two following Notes, see Article on Phonology in "Bibliotheca Sacra," Vol. 16, by B. W. Dwight.

www.ingramcontent.com/pod-product-compliance
Lightning Source LLC
LaVergne TN
LVHW011238110826
845150LV00006B/1669

9781425513702